Overcoming the Trauma of Your Motor Vehicle Accident

EDITOR-IN-CHIEF

David H. Barlow, PhD

SCIENTIFIC
ADVISORY BOARD

Anne Marie Albano, PhD

Jack M. Gorman, MD

Peter E. Nathan, PhD

Bonnie Spring, PhD

Paul Salkovskis, PhD

G. Terence Wilson, PhD

John R. Weisz, PhD

Overcoming the Trauma of Your Motor Vehicle Accident

A COGNITIVE-BEHAVIORAL TREATMENT PROGRAM

Workbook

Edward J. Hickling • Edward B. Blanchard

2006

UNIVERSITY PRESS

Oxford University Press, Inc., publishes works that further
Oxford University's objective of excellence
in research, scholarship, and education.

Oxford   New York
Auckland   Cape Town   Dar es Salaam   Hong Kong   Karachi
Kuala Lumpur   Madrid   Melbourne   Mexico City   Nairobi
New Delhi   Shanghai   Taipei   Toronto

With offices in
Argentina   Austria   Brazil   Chile   Czech Republic   France   Greece
Guatemala   Hungary   Italy   Japan   Poland   Portugal   Singapore
South Korea   Switzerland   Thailand   Turkey   Ukraine   Vietnam

Copyright © 2006 by Oxford University Press, Inc.

Published by Oxford University Press, Inc.
198 Madison Avenue, New York, New York 10016

www.oup.com

Oxford is a registered trademark of Oxford University Press

All rights reserved. No part of this publication may be reproduced,
stored in a retrieval system, or transmitted, in any form or by any means,
electronic, mechanical, photocopying, recording, or otherwise,
without the prior permission of Oxford University Press.

ISBN-13 978-0-19-530607-1

Printed in the United States of America
on acid-free paper

About Treatments That Work™

One of the most difficult problems confronting patients with various disorders and diseases is finding the best help available. Everyone is aware of friends or family who have sought treatment from a seemingly reputable practitioner, only to find out later from another doctor that the original diagnosis was wrong or that the recommended treatments were inappropriate, or perhaps even harmful. Many patients and family members address this problem by reading everything they can about their symptoms, seeking out information on the Internet, or aggressively "asking around" to tap knowledge from friends and acquaintances. Governments and health care policymakers are also aware that people in need don't always get the best treatments—something they refer to as "variability in healthcare practices."

Now health care systems around the world are attempting to correct this variability by introducing "evidence-based practice." This simply means that it is in everyone's interest that patients get the most up-to-date and effective care for a particular problem. Health care policymakers have also recognized that it is very useful to give consumers of healthcare as much information as possible, so that they can make intelligent decisions in a collaborative effort to improve health and mental health. This series, Treatments That Work™, is designed to accomplish just that. The latest and most effective interventions for particular problems are described in user-friendly language. To be included in this series, each treatment program must pass the highest standards of evidence available, as determined by a scientific advisory board. Thus, when people experiencing these problems or their family members seek out an expert clinician who is familiar with these interventions and decides that they are appropriate, they can be confident that they are receiving the best care available. Of course, only your health care professional can decide on the right treatment or combination of treatments, for you.

This particular program presents the latest version of a cognitive-behavioral treatment program for posttraumatic stress disorder due to motor vehicle accidents. Each year millions of people are injured in car accidents, and while physical injuries are usually treated promptly, the emotional aftermath can be even more disabling and can last for years, if untreated. In this program, you will learn skills to cope with and eventually master the emotional roller coaster of depression, anxiety, and sometimes anger, as well as the flashbacks that can linger for months or years after a severe trauma. This program is most effectively applied by working in collaboration with your clinician.

David H. Barlow, Editor-in-Chief,
Treatments That Work™
Boston, MA

Contents

Chapter 1   Introduction *3*

Chapter 2   Overview of the Program *9*

Chapter 3   Pretreatment Assessment *14*

Chapter 4   Session 1 *27*

Chapter 5   Session 2 *41*

Chapter 6   Session 3 *45*

Chapter 7   Session 4 *59*

Chapter 8   Session 5 *71*

Chapter 9   Midtreatment Reassessment *77*

Chapter 10   Session 6 *83*

Chapter 11   Sessions 7 Through 9 *87*

Chapter 12   End-of-Treatment Reassessment *97*

Chapter 13   Session 10: Termination Session *103*

References and Suggestions for Further Reading *105*

About the Authors *109*

Overcoming the Trauma of Your Motor Vehicle Accident

Chapter 1 *Introduction*

Case Study: Janelle

Janelle's accident happened so suddenly. She was simply making a left turn as she was leaving the shopping mall that she'd been to a hundred times before. She wasn't going that fast, when suddenly a car came from the other lane and pushed her car into a telephone pole! As the car was heading toward the pole, all Janelle could think was, "I'm going to die!" "So this is how I'm going to die!"

Janelle was hurt. Her neck was sore, and she had shooting pains in her left arm. When people came to help her, she felt dazed. But all she could think about was, if she had died, how much her daughter was going to miss her. How she wasn't going to see her granddaughter reach middle school. She'd been certain that no one could have survived that crash, yet she had!

As the weeks turned into months, she made visit after visit to doctors. She had seen her family doctor, who'd sent her to an orthopedic surgeon, who sent her to a physiatrist and then to a neurologist. She'd also seen a physical therapist and a massage therapist. The pain got somewhat better, but it didn't leave. It kept reminding her of the accident.

She was able to drive, but after 6 months, she still found it hard to go back to the mall. Thoughts of dying could come at any time, at night in her sleep, or during the day, without warning. Just like that, her old life had ended. Would she ever get it back?

Finally, when her family doctor of 20 years asked how she was doing, she burst into tears. Something had to be done!

Goals

- To understand the facts about motor vehicle accidents (MVAs)
- To understand MVA-related posttraumatic stress disorder (PTSD)
- To learn the risk factors for the development of PTSD after an MVA

The Facts About Motor Vehicle Accidents

Although precise data on the actual number of MVAs occurring in the United States are not available, it is estimated that, in any 1 year, more than 2% of the entire population has an MVA (U.S. National Highway Traffic Safety Administration, 2002). Accidents occur so often now that the majority of American men and women have at least a minor MVA by the age of 30 years.

Fortunately, fatalities from MVAs are not common. In 2000, the National Highway Traffic Safety Administration reported that there were 41,800 motor vehicle fatalities out of an estimated 3,219,000 personal injuries (U.S. National Highway Traffic Safety Administration, 2002).

The overall cost of MVAs is exorbitant. When one considers the time lost from work, the cost of care for the medical injury, and the effect on the individual's life, the overall cost is estimated to be in the tens of billions of dollars each year.

The psychological effects of an MVA can be disturbing and powerful. The emotional aftermath of a trauma, however, often is not so easy to see. Fortunately, we have begun to recognize the emotional difficulties that can follow an accident.

Case Study: Cheryl

The accident had happened weeks ago. Everyone had told her how lucky she was to be alive. She didn't even break a bone! Sure, she had some bruises where the seat belt held her tightly, but it had saved her life. The smell of the air bag and the impact of the white blur hitting her just wouldn't leave her mind. The dreams had begun almost immediately after the accident. They bothered her nearly every night, and most included a part where the car went sailing in the air off the road. She just couldn't stop it! The police officers had said that she'd hit some black ice. She never realized the black ice was there. She can still hear herself screaming, "No!!!"

The nightmares made it hard to want to go to sleep, no matter how tired she was. It seemed as if as soon as her head hit the pillow, the dreams came. They weren't always about the crash, but they were always horrible. Sometimes it was the horror of the impact, or other feelings of being out of control, or even of her actually dying. The dreams seemed to wait for her each night.

Cheryl's husband watches her closely all the time now. When they go anywhere in a car, he drives, and Cheryl clutches the door handle or wrings her hands anxiously. Sunday drives aren't fun anymore. The memory of the crash won't leave her, and it plays itself over and over in her mind. Cheryl told her friend Diane that it's as if the accident has haunted her. The images and feelings just won't leave. Sometimes she feels as if she is living on borrowed time, that she escaped this time, but she won't be as lucky the next time.

Everywhere she goes, the mistakes of other drivers are magnified. "How can such idiots be allowed to be on the roads?" "Don't they know how dangerous it is?" Life has been more limited for her ever since the accident. She doesn't do as much, and the things that once gave her joy now give her little pleasure, if any. Nothing seems to interest Cheryl as it did before, and she wonders if she'll ever feel the way she did before the accident.

What Is Posttraumatic Stress Disorder?

Posttraumatic stress disorder is categorized as an anxiety disorder, with several major conditions, or criteria, that must be met to reach a diagnosis. The major categories include experiencing a traumatic event and being very frightened by it; reexperiencing the traumatic event; avoiding subsequent events that are similar to the event or are reminders of it; numbing of feelings and responsiveness compared with what was experienced before the traumatic event; and physical hyperarousal while going through such situations.

Specific Criteria for a Diagnosis of Posttraumatic Stress Disorder

To diagnose a person with PTSD, mental health professionals use criteria set forth in the *Diagnostic and Statistical Manual of Mental Disorders,* published by the American Psychiatric Association (*DSM-IV;* APA, 1994). A complete listing of the criteria necessary to reach a diagnosis of PTSD follows.

DSM-IV Diagnostic Criteria for Posttraumatic Stress Disorder

A. The person has been exposed to a traumatic event in which both of the following were present:
   (1) The person experienced, witnessed, or was confronted with an event or events that involved actual or threatened death or serious injury, or a threat to the physical integrity of self or others.

(2) The person's response involved intense fear, helplessness, or horror. *Note:* In children, this may be expressed instead by disorganized or agitated behavior.

B. The traumatic event is persistently reexperienced in one (or more) of the following ways:
   (1) Recurrent and intrusive distressing recollections of the event, including images, thoughts, or perceptions. *Note:* In young children, repetitive play may occur in which themes or aspects of the trauma are expressed.
   (2) Recurrent distressing dreams of the event. *Note:* In children, there may be frightening dreams without recognizable content.
   (3) Acting or feeling as if the traumatic event were recurring (includes a sense of reliving the experience, illusions, hallucinations, and dissociative flashback episodes, including those that occur upon awakening or when intoxicated). *Note:* In young children, trauma-specific reenactment may occur.
   (4) Intense psychological distress at exposure to internal or external cues that symbolize or resemble an aspect of the traumatic event.
   (5) Physiological reactivity on exposure to internal or external cues that symbolize or resemble an aspect of the traumatic event.

C. Persistent avoidance of stimuli associated with the trauma and numbing of general responsiveness (not present before the trauma), as indicated by three (or more) of the following:
   (1) Efforts to avoid thoughts, feelings, or conversations associated with the trauma
   (2) Efforts to avoid activities, places, or people that arouse recollections of the trauma
   (3) Inability to recall an important aspect of the trauma
   (4) Markedly diminished interest or participation in significant activities
   (5) Feeling of detachment or estrangement from others
   (6) Restricted range of affect (e.g., unable to have loving feelings)
   (7) Sense of foreshortened future (e.g., does not expect to have a career, marriage, children, or a normal life span)

D. Persistent symptoms of increased arousal (not present before the trauma), as indicated by two (or more) of the following:
   (1) Difficulty falling or staying asleep
   (2) Irritability or outbursts of anger

(3) Difficulty concentrating
(4) Hypervigilance
(5) Exaggerated startle response

E. Duration of the disturbance (symptoms in Criteria B, C, and D) is more than 1 month.

F. The disturbance causes clinically significant distress or impairment in social, occupational, or other important areas of functioning.

Specify if:
  Acute: if duration of symptoms is less than 3 months.
  Chronic: if duration of symptoms is 3 months or more.

Specify if:
  With delayed onset: if onset of symptoms is at least 6 months after the stressor.

It is important to note that PTSD cannot be properly diagnosed until 1 month after the MVA. Sometimes, as in the case of Cheryl, symptoms occur shortly after the MVA. For some people, symptoms then begin to get better.

Comorbidity

In addition to PTSD, there are several other common problems that can follow an MVA. These include depression, travel anxiety, concerns over one's mortality and life, and anger. These issues will also be addressed in this workbook.

Who Is at Risk for Posttraumatic Stress Disorder?

Our own studies have shown that there are four independent factors that indicate an increased risk of PTSD after an MVA.

- A history of clinical (or major) depression at some point before the MVA

- The extent of physical injury

- The degree of fear of dying in the MVA

- The initiation of litigation

Risk Factors

The form below lists risk factors for PTSD. The more "yes" responses you have, the greater the likelihood that you will have PTSD after an MVA.

PTSD Risk Factors

Risk Variable	Yes	No
Did you have dissociative symptoms (out-of-body experiences, a sense of unreality, time alteration, and especially a sense of things occurring in slow motion) at the time of the accident or continuing?		
Are you reexperiencing symptoms (intrusive recollections, nightmares, flashbacks, or distress when reminded of the MVA)?		
Are you attempting to avoid thoughts or real-life reminders of the accident?		
Were your physical injuries serious?		
Did you experience extreme fright or terror at the prospect of dying during the MVA?		
Did you have a history of serious depression before the MVA?		
Were you diagnosed with PTSD before the MVA?		
Are you female?		
Was anyone killed in the MVA?		

Chapter 2 *Overview of the Program*

Goals

- To learn how this program was developed
- To determine if this treatment is right for you
- To understand what the program will involve

How Was the Program Developed?

The program to treat MVA-related PTSD was developed as part of the Albany MVA Project. The project initially studied a large number of individuals who had PTSD after an MVA (nearly 40%). Once it was established that this was a significant problem, the project naturally tried to develop treatments to help people who were affected by an MVA. After a number of pilot projects were done to study what seemed to be the most helpful procedures, a large-scale, controlled treatment program was developed and tested.

Is This Treatment Right for You?

The focus of this course of treatment is not so much on minor MVAs, or what are termed "fender benders." Instead, this treatment is used with individuals involved in MVAs that are serious enough to cause an emotional effect. We believe that most people can deal reasonably well with minor accidents that do not result in the need for medical attention. However, if you have been in a more serious accident, one that required medical care or that left you with lasting emotional effects, then this particular treatment may be effective for you.

Has This Program Been Successful?

Yes!

The Albany MVA Project conducted a randomized controlled trial comparing the Cognitive-Behavioral Therapy (CBT) treatment featured in this manual with supportive psychotherapy by very experienced therapists and with in-depth assessment and review of records, followed by a 3-month wait for treatment (wait list control). All of the patients met the criteria for MVA-related PTSD or were severely symptomatic as a result of an MVA. On average, the MVA had occurred more than a year earlier (Blanchard & Hickling, 2004).

Those receiving CBT showed significantly more improvement after an average of 10 treatment sessions (76% no longer met the criteria for PTSD) than those receiving supportive psychotherapy (48% improved) or those in the wait list control group (23% improved).

The results held up very well at follow-up assessments 1 year and 2 years after the end of treatment (Blanchard, Hickling et al., 2004). By the end of treatment, 82% of those treated with CBT no longer reported symptoms of major depression, compared with 41% of those receiving supportive psychotherapy and 30% of those in the wait list control group.

What Will the Program Involve?

Treatment typically requires 8 to 12 sessions (maybe more), with an average of 10 sessions.

The Program

This workbook and the treatment program will entail learning a number of skills that have been found to help people suffering from PTSD after an MVA. These skills include learning a number of relaxation techniques and learning different ways to think about the MVA and the reactions that followed. It will also include an exposure intervention in which you will learn how to face those things that currently provoke very uncomfortable feelings and anxiety. This will be done in a way that will let you master them and also deal with other issues, such as handling feelings of numbness and

Table 2.1 Treatment Components and Timeline

	Week 1	Week 2	Week 3	Week 4	Week 5	Week 6	Week 7–9	Week 10
Intervention	Provide psychoeducation, practice relaxation, write an MVA description (week 1), meet with the spouse or partner							
		Rate travel situations with SUDS; read the MVA description three to four times per day; practice 11-, 8-, and 4-muscle-group relaxation exercises; begin or use coping self-statements; build and apply the travel hierarchy (use as needed)						
				Begin cognitive reappraisal, continue the relaxation exercises, practice relaxation, introduce relaxation-by-recall, continue to read the MVA description, begin and continue imaginal and in vivo exposure to the travel hierarchy, continue with coping statements				
						Review all skills or tools learned up to this point; explore issues of mortality, anger, depression, or isolation (as needed)		
	Entire treatment typically takes 8 to 12 weeks							

estrangement from others, coping with anger, facing one's mortality, and managing life changes caused by the MVA, as well as issues that are perhaps unique to your response.

Table 2.1 shows the various components of your treatment and an approximate timeline for completing each one.

The workbook and its program have not been scientifically validated as a stand alone, do-it-yourself treatment program. However, anecdotally, we do know some MVA survivors who have successfully used it that way. The program has been empirically proven to work with experienced therapists. Working with a therapist is recommended and should increase the chances of gaining the results you are hoping for.

Finally we have not used this program with children or adolescents, nor has it been evaluated with patients with moderate to severe head injury at the time of the MVA (e.g., unconscious for more than a few minutes as a result of a blow to the head).

Chapter 3 *Pretreatment Assessment*

Case Study: John

John was troubled. He knew that he had changed since his accident, but he figured that it would be just a matter of time before he felt like his old self. But it was taking longer than he thought it should. Now he was having a hard time focusing his thoughts on anything. The accident kept popping into his mind at odd moments, and he couldn't seem to stop it. It was a little better than it had been in the first few weeks, but when would it stop? Sleep was a disaster. At first, he'd have trouble falling asleep. Then, if he could get to sleep, he'd be up almost every hour. His dreams were disturbing, and they made it hard for him to want to go back to sleep, even though he felt exhausted. Driving was torture. It seemed as if every driver was too close or went too fast, and somehow it seemed that the world had changed and all of the drivers were horrible. He knew that he couldn't keep forcing himself to get to work while he was feeling this way. He was feeling down and depressed. It was hard for him to force himself to keep going. He was doing it, but thank goodness, Debbie at work was pitching in and covering the things that he just couldn't seem to get to or remember to do. Should he get help? Would things get better if he just hung in there a little longer? What was wrong with him?

Goals

- To use assessment instruments to determine whether you are suffering from PTSD, travel anxiety, or depression related to your MVA

Assessment of Post–Motor Vehicle Accident Distress (or How Do I Know How I'm Doing?)

Some of the questions that many people have after an accident include, "How am I doing?" and "Are the things I'm feeling normal, or do I need help?"

This section of the book provides you with a number of questionnaires and tests that will help you to see how you are doing emotionally. We have arranged the questionnaires in the following way.

The first questionnaire assesses the symptoms of PTSD, which can be formally diagnosed 30 days after the time of the trauma. The second questionnaire assesses the presence of travel anxiety and driving phobia. Finally, the third questionnaire provides an assessment of the symptoms of depression.

It is imperative that you do not see these questionnaires as a substitute for meeting with a qualified mental health professional for the assessment and diagnosis of a disorder. The questionnaires are not provided for that purpose. They are meant to be a "psychological yardstick" to help you measure how you are doing and to provide a reference point with which you can compare your scores and items with those of other people who have also experienced an MVA trauma.

If you believe that you are feeling distressed or having difficulty, even if the scores are not in a "critical" range, please let your therapist know. If you think that you are feeling all right, but your scores fall in the range of people who have a significant reaction, please consider whether you might be minimizing, or even denying, your symptoms. If that seems possible, it is suggested that you discuss this as well with your treating mental health professional.

Please take the completed questionnaires to your first treatment session with your therapist!

Posttraumatic Stress Disorder

As you have learned, PTSD can be diagnosed only if the symptoms continue for 30 days or more after the traumatic event. PTSD can be diagnosed only if you have experienced a traumatic event. The event needs to have threatened your life or your physical well-being or caused an actual death or a serious injury. Your reaction to the trauma needs to have been one of intense fear, horror, or helplessness. You may reexperience the event in a number of ways, including intrusive thoughts, dreams, flashbacks, or distress if you find yourself in a situation that resembles the event. You may also have physical distress, such as increased heart rate, increased respiration, and increased muscle tension, when placed in a situation that reminds you of the traumatic event. Other symptoms can include avoidance and numbing, as well as increased arousal, which can include sleep disturbance, decreased concentration, irritability, and hypervigilance. For PTSD, the symptoms must have persisted for more than a month and must be distressing or have a negative impact on social or occupational functioning.

The test questionnaire that we have provided comes from leaders in PTSD research, who are based largely at the National Center for PTSD in Boston. The PTSD Checklist (PCL), developed by Weathers, Litz, Herman, Huska, and Keane (1993), is a 17-item questionnaire that asks you to rate the severity of each of the 17 symptoms of PTSD from 1 (not at all) to 5 (extremely). The maximum score is 85. We have found that a score of 44 or higher has great predictive capability for identifying the presence of PTSD in people who have had an MVA. We have also found that in individuals who have a score as high as 55 there is an increased likelihood that they will continue to have PTSD as long as 2 years later.

Case Study: Mary

The day had begun like any other. Mary was on her way to work early in the morning. She had many things on her mind that morning, the morning her accident occurred. The first thing she saw was a huge shadow that came over her; her next memory was the sound of squealing brakes. Then there was a huge impact. Mary awakened in a daze. She was unsure how long she had been lying there. She saw that the contents of her purse had been scattered around the car. Mary's next memory was of someone talking to her. He didn't make sense. She didn't know who he was or why he was there. It was hard to see. She could taste blood dripping into her mouth. The taste of the blood made her sick to her stomach. She remembers hearing someone say, "Are you all right? Are you all right?" She drifted in and out of awareness for a while, and then she heard a police officer say, "Just lie still. We'll have you out of there soon."

Then it dawned on her. She'd been in a terrible crash, and she was hurt! After that, it was a blur. Mary moved in and out of awareness. She next remembered being at a hospital, with doctors asking a lot of questions and ordering tests. She was scared about what would happen next. All she could think was, "I could have died!" "I didn't do anything wrong!" "How could this have happened to me?"

About 2 months after her accident, Mary completed the questionnaire as to how she had been feeling over the past month (figure 3.1). On one item, feeling as if her future would be cut short, she replied "not at all." When her scores are totaled, we find that she had a tally of 8 for items she felt "a little bit," 12 for items she felt "moderately," 24 for items she felt "quite a bit," and 10 for the two items she felt "extremely." This resulted in a total score of 55. This score is above the level that predicts PTSD (44 or higher), making it likely that she is experiencing PTSD. Her score of 55 is similar to that of the group that is likely to have PTSD 2 years later if left untreated. Mary would benefit from seeking help.

If your MVA occurred more than 30 days ago, take a moment to complete your own PTSD Checklist (page 18).

A caution is given regarding this test; if you have low scores, please see if the symptoms you have are negatively affecting your life. If they are, you may want to do some of the things that can help. If the particular symptom or symptoms you have are affecting your life, such as not getting enough sleep or finding that driving is difficult in your daily life, treatment can make a huge difference. If your scores are consistent with PTSD, then the program is designed for this disorder in particular.

Travel Anxiety

Case Study: Paula

Paula remembered her first car vividly, a red Mustang convertible. She loved to drive! Paula was always the one who picked up her friends and drove to the beach, the store, or wherever they were going. Then she had her accident. Now, her love of driving is gone. In fact, it's closer to torture for her to get behind the wheel and go anywhere. Yes, she'll drive to work and home afterward. She will drive to the doctor's office and to the store for essentials. But now, she feels scared and anxious. She had once loved to drive! No matter how much she tells herself that her feelings are unreasonable, they don't go away. Some times and places are worse than others. Now, she dreads rush hour and bad weather. When there is rain or snow, Paula experiences near panic or refuses to drive at all. Riding in a car isn't any better, but at least when she's behind the wheel, she knows what she's going to do next.

Figure 3.1 Current Posttraumatic Stress Disorder Checklist (PCL)

Name: Mary   Date: _____

Instructions: Following is a list of problems and complaints that people sometimes have in response to stressful life experiences (i.e., your most distressing MVA). Please read each one carefully, and then circle one of the numbers to the right to indicate how much you were bothered by that problem *in the past month*.

	Not at All	**A Little Bit**	**Moderately**	**Quite a Bit**	**Extremely**
1. Repeated, disturbing memories, thoughts, or images of the stressful experience?	1	2	3	(4)	5
2. Repeated, disturbing dreams of the stressful experience?	1	2	(3)	4	5
3. Suddenly acting or feeling as if the stressful experience were happening again (as if you were reliving it)?	1	(2)	3	4	5
4. Feeling very upset when something reminded you of the stressful experience?	1	2	3	4	(5)
5. Having a physical reaction (e.g., heart pounding, trouble breathing, sweating) when something reminded you of the stressful experience?	1	2	3	(4)	5
6. Avoiding thinking about or talking about your stressful experience or avoiding having feelings related to it?	1	2	(3)	4	5
7. Avoiding activities or situations because they reminded you of your stressful experience?	1	2	3	4	(5)
8. Trouble remembering important parts of the stressful experience?	1	(2)	3	4	5
9. Loss of interest in activities that you used to enjoy?	1	2	3	(4)	5
10. Feeling distant or cut off from others?	1	(2)	3	4	5
11. Feeling emotionally numb or being unable to have loving feelings for those close to you?	1	(2)	3	4	5
12. Feeling as if your future somehow will be cut short?	(1)	2	3	4	5
13. Trouble falling or staying asleep?	1	2	3	(4)	5
14. Feeling irritable or having angry outbursts?	1	2	3	(4)	5
15. Having difficulty concentrating?	1	2	(3)	4	5
16. Being "super-alert," watchful, or on guard?	1	2	3	(4)	5
17. Feeling jumpy or easily startled?	1	2	(3)	4	5
Total	1	8	12	24	10

Current Posttraumatic Stress Disorder Checklist (PCL)

Name: _____   Date: _____

Instructions: Following is a list of problems and complaints that people sometimes have in response to stressful life experiences (i.e., your most distressing MVA). Please read each one carefully, and then circle one of the numbers to the right to indicate how much you were bothered by that problem *in the past month*.

	Not at All	A Little Bit	Moderately	Quite a Bit	Extremely
1. Repeated, disturbing memories, thoughts, or images of the stressful experience?	1	2	3	4	5
2. Repeated, disturbing dreams of the stressful experience?	1	2	3	4	5
3. Suddenly acting or feeling as if the stressful experience were happening again (as if you were reliving it)?	1	2	3	4	5
4. Feeling very upset when something reminded you of the stressful experience?	1	2	3	4	5
5. Having a physical reaction (e.g., heart pounding, trouble breathing, sweating) when something reminded you of the stressful experience?	1	2	3	4	5
6. Avoiding thinking about or talking about your stressful experience or avoiding having feelings related to it?	1	2	3	4	5
7. Avoiding activities or situations because they reminded you of your stressful experience?	1	2	3	4	5
8. Trouble remembering important parts of the stressful experience?	1	2	3	4	5
9. Loss of interest in activities that you used to enjoy?	1	2	3	4	5
10. Feeling distant or cut off from others?	1	2	3	4	5
11. Feeling emotionally numb or being unable to have loving feelings for those close to you?	1	2	3	4	5
12. Feeling as if your future somehow will be cut short?	1	2	3	4	5
13. Trouble falling or staying asleep?	1	2	3	4	5
14. Feeling irritable or having angry outbursts?	1	2	3	4	5
15. Having difficulty concentrating?	1	2	3	4	5
16. Being "super-alert," watchful, or on guard?	1	2	3	4	5
17. Feeling jumpy or easily startled?	1	2	3	4	5
Total					

It is very common for anyone who has been in an MVA to have some anxiety or discomfort when driving. In its worst form, this can result in a panic attack. A panic attack is a very intense period of anxiety that can include symptoms such as heart palpitations or accelerated heart rate, sweating, trembling or shaking, shortness of breath, feeling as if you're choking, chest pain or discomfort, nausea or stomach distress, dizziness or feeling faint, numbing or tingling sensations in the arms or legs, and hot flashes or chills. Panic attacks can also include feelings of unreality or feeling detached from oneself, fear of losing control or going crazy, and a fear of dying.

Anxiety related to driving can take many forms. It can be a physical sensation that is described as a state of tension or muscular tightness; it can also be a feeling of fear or apprehension that something is about to occur. Whatever the feeling, it can affect your driving.

Driving can be limited in a couple of ways. Some people avoid it outright, simply refusing to drive. This can lead to the need to rely on others to drive or the need to take public transportation in a person who formerly drove himself or herself. Driving can often be avoided. For example, you may not drive in certain places (e.g., the scene of the accident, major highways, congested roads), or you may avoid certain weather or driving conditions (e.g., darkness, unfamiliar places, bad weather). Being a passenger is often even worse than being the driver. When you're driving, at least you have some control. When you're a passenger, you're "out of control" and totally "at the mercy of the driver" and his or her skills and reactions.

The Travel Anxiety Questionnaire (TAQ) addresses a number of these concerns in a self-report format (see page 22). This questionnaire looks at specific areas of driving behavior that may have been negatively affected by the MVA. Although the score of the questionnaire is obtained for both the degree of avoidance and the amount of anxiety experienced, there are no critical levels that indicate the presence or absence of travel anxiety. For some items (e.g., driving in snow), the answers are dependent on where you live, because some places never or only rarely see snow. So, although the score itself is not critical, the more items that show problem areas, the more driving has been negatively affected. The areas of difficulty that are identified may suggest specific targeted areas for intervention as part of your treatment.

For example, figure 3.2 shows the TAQ for Paula. Paula is still driving, but as you can see, she has a great deal of distress when she does. She finds it hard to drive in certain traffic conditions (at night, in heavy traffic) and in certain weather conditions (snow, rain), and she no longer enjoys taking pleasure trips or riding as a passenger in a car. Clearly, the MVA has affected her current driving. She now experiences a level of anxiety and discomfort that was not present prior to her accident. Paula is experiencing many of the symptoms that have been shown to improve with the type of treatment outlined in the next section.

Depression

As you have learned, depression can often follow an MVA. Life can be dramatically changed when you have been in a traumatic car crash. Emotionally, you may feel awful. Thoughts of the MVA may disturb you. Your sleep may be affected. You might be out of work. You might be receiving physical therapy. You may have injuries that don't seem to get better, no matter what you try. Before you even realize it, your mood may also be changing.

Depression is a mood disorder, in which you feel sad almost every day for 2 weeks or more. You may also lose interest in, or no longer enjoy, things that once brought you pleasure. To meet the criterion for clinical depression, depressed mood must be present most of the day, nearly every day. Other symptoms can include significant weight loss (or weight gain), sleep disturbance (either too little or too much), agitation or slowing of activity, fatigue or loss of energy nearly every day, feelings of worthlessness or excessive guilt, diminished ability to think or concentrate, and recurrent thoughts of death or suicidal ideation. These symptoms affect social, occupational, or other important areas of functioning.

To help in the assessment of depression, we have provided the Depression Scale that was developed by the Center for Epidemiologic Studies (CES-D) (Radloff, 1977). This scale allows us to quantify the severity of depressive symptoms by allowing you to total the number of items that reflect how you're feeling. The CES-D is a 20-item, self-report measure of depression. It was derived from a number of longer psychological instruments to assess depression in the general population, with an emphasis on depressed mood. Individuals are asked to rate how each of the 20 items has applied to them over the past 2 weeks, using a 0- to 3-point scale, where 0 = "rarely or none of the time," 1 = "some or a little of the time," 2 = "occasionally or a moderate amount of the time," and 3 = "most or all of the time."

Figure 3.2 Travel Anxiety Questionnaire (TAQ)

Name: Paula _____ Date: _____

1. Are you driving at the **present** time? (Circle one)
   1. (Yes) Go to question 3
   2. No Continue to question 2

2. If you are *not* driving presently, why not?
   (Check *all* that apply)
   - ☐ Driving makes me anxious
   - ☐ Physically unable
   - ☐ No car
   - ☐ No license
   - ☐ None of the above

3. Following are eight driving situations. Use the two scales below to **rate how anxious** you are about each situation currently, as well as **how much you avoid** each of these situations **currently.** If the situation does not apply to you, please circle "NA" next to the situation.

   Anxiety Rating Scale

0	1	2	3	4
No anxiety	Very little anxiety	Some anxiety	Moderate anxiety	Severe anxiety

   Avoidance Rating Scale

0	1	2	3	4
None of the time	Less than half of the time	About half of the time	More than half of the time	All of the time

	Anxiety rating	Avoidance rating	
Driving at night	3	3	NA
Driving in snow			(NA)
Driving in rain	4	2	NA
Highway driving	2	1	NA
Driving in heavy traffic	4	4	NA
Driving in the location of the MVA	4	2	NA
Driving on pleasure trips	2	4	NA
Being the passenger	4	4	NA

Please circle either yes or no:

4. **Currently,** do you restrict your driving speed? (Yes) No

5. **Currently,** do you drive only to work? Yes (No)

Travel Anxiety Questionnaire (TAQ)

Name: _____   Date: _____

1. Are you driving at the **present** time? (Circle one)
   1. Yes   Go to question 3
   2. No   Continue to question 2

2. If you are *not* driving presently, why not? (Check *all* that apply)
   - ☐ Driving makes me anxious
   - ☐ Physically unable
   - ☐ No car
   - ☐ No license
   - ☐ None of the above

3. Following are eight driving situations. Use the two scales below to **rate how anxious** you are about each situation currently, as well as **how much you avoid** each of these situations **currently**. If the situation does not apply to you, please circle "NA" next to the situation.

   Anxiety Rating Scale

0	1	2	3	4
No anxiety	Very little anxiety	Some anxiety	Moderate anxiety	Severe anxiety

   Avoidance Rating Scale

0	1	2	3	4
None of the time	Less than half of the time	About half of the time	More than half of the time	All of the time

	Anxiety rating	Avoidance rating	
Driving at night	_____	_____	NA
Driving in snow	_____	_____	NA
Driving in rain	_____	_____	NA
Highway driving	_____	_____	NA
Driving in heavy traffic	_____	_____	NA
Driving in the location of the MVA	_____	_____	NA
Driving on pleasure trips	_____	_____	NA
Being the passenger	_____	_____	NA

Please circle either yes or no:

4. **Currently,** do you restrict your driving speed?   Yes   No

5. **Currently,** do you drive only to work?   Yes   No

The CES-D is scored by summing, or adding up, all of the items. In most populations, a score of 16 or higher is consistent with depression. The higher the score you obtain, the more likely it is that you would meet the criteria for depression. In addition to the 20 items on the CES-D, we added 2 more. These items reflect thoughts of death and harming oneself. They are important but do not add to the total score. Please put a checkmark in the category that best fits how you feel. Obviously, some items, such as the presence of suicidal ideation, warrant immediate medical attention.

Although we have great confidence that the information in this book has the potential to help many people, when a person is troubled by thoughts that could lead to risking his or her life or safety, prompt action by professionals is needed. Please use your judgment and obtain help immediately if you feel so depressed that it is affecting your will to live. Take a moment to complete the CES-D (page 25).

Many of the symptoms of depression can overlap with the symptoms of PTSD. The information in the treatment section has been found to help people who are suffering from what is called "dual diagnoses," or having both PTSD and major depression. However, that help was provided by trained professionals who were able to monitor how each individual was progressing in treatment. No treatment has the ability to help everyone.

An explanation of how to understand the CES-D is provided in the example of Cheryl (figure 3.3). Cheryl took the test by answering the questions as to how she felt over the past 2 weeks. She then added up the items. Her total score was 21. This is above the range for suggesting that she is experiencing major depression. It would be our recommendation that she contact her physician or a mental health professional. This decision is particularly important when one considers that the risk of death through suicide needs careful assessment and that help is available. The last two items added to the version of the CES-D included in this workbook are intended to assess the occurrence of thoughts about death and thoughts about harming oneself. They are not added to the total score, but clearly are important. If Cheryl's responses had indicated that she had frequent or strong thoughts about death or harming herself, it would be our recommendation that she immediately seek help from a local medical or mental health professional. Our experience in a clinic setting has been that depression, particularly mild depression, can improve with the treatment offered in this book.

Figure 3.3 Current Center for Epidemiologic Studies–Depression (CES-D)

Name: _Cheryl_____ Date: _____

For each statement, please circle the number that best describes how often you have felt or behaved this way during the **past two weeks**.

	Rarely or None of the Time	Some or a Little of the Time	Occasionally or a Moderate Amount of the Time	Most or All of the Time
I was bothered by things that usually don't bother me	0	(1)	2	3
I did not feel like eating; my appetite was poor	0	(1)	2	3
I felt like I could not shake off the blues, even with help from my family or friends	0	1	(2)	3
I felt like I was just as good as other people	(0)	1	2	3
I had trouble keeping my mind on what I was doing	0	(1)	2	3
I felt depressed	0	1	(2)	3
I felt that everything I did was an effort	0	(1)	2	3
I felt hopeful about the future	(0)	1	2	3
I thought my life had been a failure	(0)	1	2	3
I felt fearful	0	(1)	2	3
My sleep was restless	0	1	2	(3)
I was happy	0	1	(2)	3
I talked less than usual	0	(1)	2	3
I felt lonely	(0)	1	2	3
People were unfriendly	(0)	1	2	3
I enjoyed life	0	(1)	2	3
I had crying spells	0	1	(2)	3
I felt sad	0	1	(2)	3
I felt like people disliked me	(0)	1	2	3
I could not get "going"*	0	(1)	2	3
I had thoughts about my death	0	(1)	2	3
I thought about harming myself	(0)	1	2	3
Sum of scores	0	8	10	3
Total score = 21				

*Stop scoring after this item.

Current Center for Epidemiologic Studies–Depression (CES-D)

Name: _____ Date: _____

For each statement, please circle the number that best describes how often you have felt or behaved this way during the **past two weeks.**

	Rarely or None of the Time	Some or a Little of the Time	Occasionally or a Moderate Amount of the Time	Most or All of the Time
I was bothered by things that usually don't bother me	0	1	2	3
I did not feel like eating; my appetite was poor	0	1	2	3
I felt like I could not shake off the blues, even with help from my family or friends	0	1	2	3
I felt like I was just as good as other people	0	1	2	3
I had trouble keeping my mind on what I was doing	0	1	2	3
I felt depressed	0	1	2	3
I felt that everything I did was an effort	0	1	2	3
I felt hopeful about the future	0	1	2	3
I thought my life had been a failure	0	1	2	3
I felt fearful	0	1	2	3
My sleep was restless	0	1	2	3
I was happy	0	1	2	3
I talked less than usual	0	1	2	3
I felt lonely	0	1	2	3
People were unfriendly	0	1	2	3
I enjoyed life	0	1	2	3
I had crying spells	0	1	2	3
I felt sad	0	1	2	3
I felt like people disliked me	0	1	2	3
I could not get "going"*	0	1	2	3
I had thoughts about my death	0	1	2	3
I thought about harming myself	0	1	2	3
Sum of scores				
Total score =				

*Stop scoring after this item.

Chapter 4 *Session 1*

Overview

Session 1 begins with a review of the assessments that you completed earlier (chapter 3). Your therapist will go over your results with you and provide an overview of PTSD and how stress reactions to a traumatic event occur (see chapters 1 and 2). This information is provided as a starting point to help you understand much of what has happened and why.

You should practice the initial relaxation exercise twice a day, for at least 2 weeks. Rate your depth of relaxation each time, so that you can chart your progress.

In your first session, you are given the assignment to write a detailed description of your MVA. Try to complete the description by session 2.

Goals

- To review your completed pretreatment assessments
- To review information found in chapters 1 and 2 of this workbook
- To learn the initial relaxation technique
- To begin practicing relaxation twice a day, every day
- To monitor your progress using the relaxation rating scale
- To write a description of your MVA

Initial Relaxation Training Exercise

Relaxation training consists of teaching you how to relax your muscles very systematically by tensing and then relaxing the major muscle groups of the body, helping you to recognize how it feels to be relaxed, and then teaching you ways to bring on those feelings of relaxation very quickly and very reliably through a series of exercises. One key to this exercise is to pay careful attention to each of the sensations that you associate with a subjective sense of relaxation. With practice, you will be able to learn to become deeply relaxed very quickly. This will become very important because, once you learn how to relax very quickly, you will be able to apply this skill in situations that, at this point, provoke a sense of anxiety (such as driving). If you can counter the feelings of anxiety with relaxation, you will be able to put yourself into stressful situations and tolerate them much more easily, thereby setting the stage to master those situations.

We have found that the optimum schedule for learning relaxation is to practice twice per day. It is certainly possible to practice more than twice per day, and you may find more frequent practice to be of benefit, in terms of both how you feel and how readily you learn. Learning how to relax takes time, and it is a skill that needs time to be developed through systematic, regular practice.

You may well have suffered a physical injury from the accident. When you read the exercises, one of the instructions will be to tense and then relax your muscles systematically. If you are asked to tense an injured muscle group, we ask you to use your own judgment about how hard you tense those muscles, if you tense them at all. The tensing itself is not as important as learning the contrast that comes during the relaxation response. Research has shown that, by tensing and relaxing muscles, you create a real physiological change in the muscles and thereby learn how the muscles feel as they hold tension and as they stretch and become relaxed, much like an athlete warms and lengthens muscles by stretching.

The setting for relaxation is important. Ideally, you should find a nice, comfortable position, either in a recliner, in your bed, or in a chair, comfortably propped with pillows. Be sure there is support for your head and neck. If you wear glasses or contact lenses, please remove them, and loosen any tight clothing that you may be wearing. When prompted, you should be tensing the muscles and holding the tension for about 5 to 10 seconds. You should tense the muscles hard enough to be aware of how they feel when they are tense. However, do not strain or hurt any muscle. If you tense too hard, you might cause more pain and aggravate a physical injury. That is certainly not something that is desired or helpful. Therefore, if it hurts when you tense, stop tensing. The goal is to create enough tension that you will experience a clear difference between tensing and relaxation.

The sequence of muscles to be tensed in the initial, long relaxation program is outlined as follows:

11-Muscle-Group Relaxation Exercise

- Right hand and lower arm
- Right upper arm
- Left hand and lower arm
- Left upper arm
- Forehead and eyes
- Lower face and jaw
- Neck and shoulders
- Chest and upper back
- Abdomen and lower back
- Hips, buttocks, and upper legs (right and left)
- Lower legs and feet

11-Muscle-Group Relaxation Script

To begin, find a comfortable position. Please be sure to find a comfortable, quiet place, where you won't be interrupted. To start, gently close your eyes and take a breath. Take a gentle breath in. Hold it, just for a moment, and then relax. Feel the difference. You body tenses slightly as you hold a breath, and then it lets go as you exhale. Find a rhythm that's right for you. Just let the air flow in and out. You may find, as you relax, that your breathing slows down. If it does, just let it happen, and feel the change, as we begin now to focus on the muscles.

Start by making a fist with your right hand. Feel the tension in your hand, across your fingers, your thumb, and your wrist, and into your lower arm. Focus on how the tension feels. Notice the tautness in your fingers, thumb, and wrist. Feel the tension in every fiber, notice all the tension . . . and then relax. Feel the difference. Your fingers may tingle and feel warm. Focus on the change. Some people find that their muscles feel warm and heavy as the relaxation enters. Some find that their muscles grow light as the tension leaves. Notice how it feels for you, and store those feelings away. Contrast how the muscles felt when they were tight . . . and how they feel now, as they let go. Imagine that a wave of relaxation has washed up your arm, touching every muscle and deepening the relaxation. Then imagine that the wave is ebbing away, taking with it all of the tension. Feel the difference, and store those feelings away. Now we move our attention up to the muscles of the upper arm.

Raise your right hand up to touch your shoulder, and then tense the muscles of your upper arm, the biceps and triceps. Feel the tension in these long muscles of the upper arm. Imagine that a band or belt has been pulled tightly around your upper arm, creating tension. Focus on that tension, noticing how every fiber, every muscle feels . . . and then relax. Feel the difference. Notice the contrast between how the muscles felt when they were tight and how they feel now, as they relax. Imagine that the feeling of relaxation has spread up your hand and lower arm, and now is entering your upper arm. Your arm feels heavy . . . warm. Focus on the change. Feel the wave of relaxation washing up your arm, and then ebbing away, bringing deep, complete relaxation. Store those feelings away. Calm. . . . Quiet. . . . Focus on the difference between how the muscles felt when they were tight and how they feel when they are relaxed. Warm . . . heavy. Allowing these feelings to grow without any thought, we'll move our attention across to the left side, starting with the left hand and lower arm.

Make a fist now with your left hand. Feel the tension in your hand, across your fingers, your thumb, and your wrist, and into your lower arm. Focus on how the tension feels. Notice the tautness again in your fingers, thumb, and wrist. Feel the tension in every fiber, and then relax. Feel the difference. The fingers may tingle and feel warm. Focus on the change. Notice how it feels for you, and store those feelings away. Contrast how the muscles felt when they were tight and how they feel now, as they let go. . . . Imagine that a wave of relaxation has again washed up your arm, touching every muscle, but now it's on the left side, deepening the relaxation. Then imagine that the wave is ebbing away, taking with it all of the tension. Feel the difference, and store those feelings away. Now we move our attention up to the muscles of the upper arm.

Raise your left hand up to touch your shoulder, and then tense the muscles of your upper arm, the biceps and triceps. Feel the tension on this side, in these long muscles of the upper arm. Imagine that a band or belt has been pulled tightly around the left upper arm, creating tension. Focus on that tension, noticing how every fiber, every tendon, every muscle feels. Then relax . . . deeply. Feel the difference. Notice the contrast between how the muscles felt when they were tight and how they feel now, as they relax. Imagine that the feeling of relaxation has spread up your hand and lower arm, and now is entering your upper arm. Heavy . . . warm. Focus on the change. Feel the wave of relaxation washing up your arm, and then ebbing away . . . bringing deep, complete relaxation. Store those feelings away. Calm . . . quiet. Focus on the difference between how the muscles felt when they were tight and how they feel now, when they are relaxed. Warm . . . heavy. Now we move our attention up to the muscles of your face and shoulders.

Let's start with the muscles of your forehead and eyes. Begin to press down with the muscles of your forehead, really tightening your brow and squinting your eyes. Feel all of the tension around your eyes. You have a lot of muscles in this area that allow you to make facial expressions. Feel every muscle. Feel the tension in your forehead, pulling on your temples and around your eyes, even pulling on your scalp . . . and then relax. Let all of the tension go, and focus on the difference. The forehead actually grows longer as it becomes less constricted, more relaxed. It may tingle and feel warm. Notice whatever changes are occurring, and store them away. Feel your eyes relax as the tension lets go and the relaxation deepens and grows. More and more relaxed. Contrast how the muscles felt when they were tight and how they feel now . . . relaxed and calm. Remember those feelings as we move our attention down to your cheeks and jaw.

What I'd like you to do is to bite down with your back teeth and pull the corners of your mouth out, making a tight grimace, a really tight face. If possible, I'd also like you to take your tongue and press it into the roof of your mouth or your front teeth. Hold that tension, feel where the tightness is . . . hold it . . . then relax. Just let go. Let all of the tension leave, and focus on the difference. If the jaw is relaxed all the way, it actually hangs open a little bit, because there's not even enough tension to hold the jaw together. Just let go, completely relaxed. Remember those feelings . . . how your jaw felt when it was tight and how it feels now, when it is relaxed. All of the muscles of your face are relaxing now . . . your forehead . . . your eyes . . . your cheeks . . . and your jaw. Completely relaxed. Now we move our attention down to the muscles of the neck and shoulders.

Again, remember, if you've injured any part of your body, don't aggravate the injury by tensing the muscles so much that they hurt. It's not necessary. Just be aware of how tension feels and especially how the muscles feel when the tension goes away. That's the memory we want to help you build.

To start, gently press your head back, tensing the muscles in the back of your neck. At the same time, raise your shoulders, making the muscles feel as if there's a knot, as they work against each other. Hold that tightness, and be aware of how the muscles feel tight and hard. Notice where the tension is, feel the tightness . . . then relax. Just let go. Let your head find a comfortable position, resting gently, with no tension holding it up. Let your shoulders relax. Just let the muscles go, loose and calm. Sagging . . . warm and comfortable. Now you should be feeling totally relaxed, letting the warm, comfortable feeling just flow into the area, without any effort at all. Now we move our attention down to the muscles of your chest and upper back.

Here, we're going to create tension a little bit differently. When we start, I'd like you to take a breath and hold it, and then relax when you exhale. When you're ready, take a deep breath, hold it, and then tense the muscles of your chest and upper back. Hold your breath, and feel the tightness of your muscles. A lot of tension is held in this region. Be aware of how the tightness feels and where it is, and then relax. Just exhale, and let all of the tension out. Let your next breath in . . . a slow, comfortable cleansing breath. Let the fresh, clean air in, and as you exhale, let all of the tension leave. You're growing calmer and more deeply relaxed with every breath. Calm . . . peaceful.

Now we move our attention down to the muscles of the stomach and lower back. Here, as with the chest, tense your muscles as you take a breath, hold the breath, and then relax as you exhale. When you're ready, take a deep breath, and as you fill your lungs, press your stomach out, distending it away from your back, feeling the tightness in your abdomen, the sides of your stomach, and even your lower back. Hold the breath, feeling the tautness in your muscles, in the whole trunk region . . . then relax. Just let your breath out, and as you do, let your chest and stomach collapse. As you take your next breath, feel the fresh air fill your lungs, and allow your stomach to rise and fall with your chest. Easily, effortlessly, rising and falling. Each time you exhale, feel your body sink deeply into the cushions. Just let go. Let all of your muscles go limp and loose. Let the cushions hold you, without any effort. As you feel your chest and stomach rise gently, much like an infant who breathes without any tension, feel the relaxation spread into your whole upper body.

Calm, peaceful, and deeply relaxed. Think the word "relax" each time you exhale, and feel your body just letting go, with no effort at all. Next we move our attention down to the muscles of your hips and upper legs.

Here, just as when we started, just tighten and relax your muscles, focusing on the contrast between how the muscles feel when they are tight and how they feel as you relax. Start by tightening your hips, your buttocks, and the muscles of your upper legs, the quads and hamstrings. Feel the tautness as you tighten you hips and upper legs. Feel the tightness . . . the tension . . . and hold it. Then relax. Just let go. Feel the change. Again, it may feel as if a warm, comfortable wave has spread over your muscles. As the tension leaves, let yourself sink into the cushions. Imagine the wave of relaxation spreading over the region, and then, as it ebbs away, taking all of the tension with it. Now we move our attention down to your lower legs and feet.

Start here by curling your toes up, creating tension in your toes, the balls of your feet, your ankles, and your calves, on both the right and the left sides. Hold the tension, feel the tightness, and notice how every fiber feels. Then let go. Just relax completely. Imagine all of the tension flowing down and out of your legs, as the relaxation washes up, warm and full, deepening the feeling of calm in every muscle. Just let go, and focus on the change, the contrast between tension and relaxation. Store those feelings away. Remember how they feel, and store that muscle memory away.

Now we're going to go through each muscle group a second time, but this time, we're not going to tighten the muscles. This time, just try to relax your muscles that extra little bit, whenever the muscle is mentioned. Starting where we left off, with the muscles of the feet and lower legs, you feel relaxed . . . quiet.

Upper legs and hips . . . calm . . . comfortable.

Stomach and lower back . . . relaxed. Your breathing is calm and peaceful.

Chest and upper back . . . quiet . . . warm . . . heavy.

Shoulders and neck . . . loose . . . and calm.

Face, down your forehead, across your eyes, down your cheeks and jaw . . . loose . . . heavy.

Then your arms, down your upper arms, your lower arms . . . and out your hands and fingers . . . calm . . . peaceful.

Now, in your mind, go through your entire body, focusing on relaxation. If you feel that any muscle group can relax more, try to focus on that group and deepen the relaxation. . . . No effort, just quiet and calm. Then, focus on the next five breaths. Just focus on taking a gentle, calm breath. As you inhale, with each breath, count from one to five, and then, as you exhale, think the word "relax." Notice yourself growing calmer and more relaxed with each breath. Take a moment to enjoy those sensations.

In a moment, it will be time to come back from this state of relaxation. To do that, you'll count back in you mind from three to one. With each number, you'll find yourself growing more alert, but still remaining very calm and comfortable. Three. You're still very calm and comfortable. Two. You're feeling a little more alert, moving around just a bit, and growing more aware. One. lowly opening your eyes and feeling alert, yet still very calm and peaceful.

As you practice this exercise, you'll find that your relaxation will deepen and begin to occur sooner.

Relaxation Rating Scale

Page 35 shows a form that can be used to record your relaxation practice sessions. You may photocopy this form or download multiple copies from the Treatments That Work™ Web site at www.oup.com/us/ttw.

Memories of the Motor Vehicle Accident

Our studies have shown that, if you can expose yourself regularly to memories and reminders of your MVA, then you can begin the process of improvement. The easiest way we have found to do this is to have you write a very complete description (in your own words) of exactly what happened at the time of the accident. In addition to the facts of the accident (similar to a police report), your description should include what happened, where it happened, and what your thoughts were as it happened. You should write as complete a description of the event as you can. In particular, this description should include your memories, including images, sights, sounds, and smells, as well as any other details of the accident that stand out.

Relaxation Rating Scale

Write in the date and check each box under the date whenever you practice the relaxation exercise. It is often helpful to rate how relaxed you are at the end of the exercise. Use a scale of 0 to 10, where you rate 0 if you are not relaxed and 10 if you are the most relaxed possible. The first exercise is the first time you practice during the day; the second is the next time you practice on the same day.

	Week 1	Week 2	Week 3	Week 4
Date				
First relaxation exercise				
Second relaxation exercise				

0 = Not at all relaxed
10 = Most relaxed you can imagine

My Motor Vehicle Accident Description

Write or type a two- to three-page description of your MVA. Be sure to include a chronological account of the accident, including what happened and what you saw, felt, heard, and smelled. Include the date, the events that led up to the MVA, and what you experienced, as well as any thoughts or images that stand out.

Pay as much attention as possible to every detail so that you can describe what you experienced, your reactions (especially your thoughts and feelings), and the actions that took place. Be sure to include what led up to the accident, what occurred during the accident, and any subsequent details, all in as much detail as possible. Try to write a description that is two to three pages long, and take it with you to your next session. This is not an assignment for an English class, so you do not need to be concerned with punctuation or grammar.

Homework

- Practice the initial relaxation technique two times a day, and record your level of relaxation.
- Write out a description of your MVA and bring it to session 2.

Homework Diary

Use the Homework Diary form from page 39 to track your homework assignments for each session. This form can be photocopied or downloaded from the Treatments That Work™ Web site at www.oup.com/us/ttw.

Homework Diary

	Monday	**Tuesday**	**Wednesday**	**Thursday**	**Friday**	**Saturday**	**Sunday**
Activity/date							
Relaxation practice							
First exercise: Relaxation rating (0–10)							
Second Exercise: Relaxation rating (0–10)							
Read the MVA description aloud (How many times?)							
Travel behavior attempted (check if yes)							
Subjective Units of Discomfort (SUDS) (before/after)							
Travel behavior attempted							
Subjective Units of Discomfort (SUDS) (before/after)							
Pleasurable activity attempted (check if yes)							
Other							

Relaxation rating: 0 = not relaxed; 10 = extremely relaxed. SUDS rating (Subjective Units of Discomfort): 0 = not at all distressed, 100 = extremely distressed, panic.

Chapter 5   *Session 2*

Overview

The description of your MVA that you wrote after session 1 will be reviewed in this session, and as homework, you will be asked to read it aloud several times a day on your own. You will also review your initial discussion of the normal reactions to trauma and PTSD (chapters 1 and 2) and continue to practice the 11-muscle-group relaxation technique.

Goals

- To review your homework records from the previous session
- To begin reading your description of your MVA daily
- To learn about avoidance and how it relates to PTSD
- To continue to practice the relaxation technique
- To identify exercises for home practice

Records Review

Before we start to cover new material, it is important to check on your progress up to this point.

You should be finding the relaxation exercise easier to use than you did the first time you tried it. You also might find that the relaxation response is happening sooner, and the exercise may leave you feeling more deeply relaxed than it did when you first tried it.

Reading and Elaboration of the Motor Vehicle Accident Description

At this time, you will review the written description of your MVA that was assigned in session 1 and read it aloud. If it seems as if there are places in your story where you are skipping over important aspects of the accident, and you can provide additional details, please add them. It is important to include as much detail as possible about your injuries, your pain, the long-term consequences of the MVA, the effects of the loss of your vehicle, and your continued physical problems, as well as your thoughts and fears, as you read the description aloud. This process of reading and remembering the accident is extremely important to a full recovery.

Now that you have written the description of your MVA and practiced reading it aloud a few times, you should begin reading it aloud three to four times a day, every day. It has been found that it is very important for you to read the description aloud, not silently. Reading the description aloud ensures that you do not skip over important parts of the trauma. Also, hearing the story as you read it aloud is another way to confront the memory (see it, hear it, and think it as a memory).

Discussion of Avoidance

At this point in the session, your therapist will review with you the information on PTSD and reactions to trauma from chapter 1 of this workbook. Again, it is important to note that avoidance of feared situations is normal. You will be asked to face these feared situations gradually, in small, manageable steps. To persevere and confront difficult aspects of PTSD symptoms while driving in anxiety-producing conditions and places, you will need to rely on both your own fortitude and the skills you will be learning in the treatment sessions.

Involvement of Significant Family Member(s)

You are encouraged to bring your spouse or partner with you to the next session (session 3). Your therapist will give your spouse or partner a general explanation of anxiety and describe how avoidance symptoms develop. This will allow your partner to more easily understand your ongoing homework, especially the exposure exercises. You will begin to expose yourself to feared situations only after you have learned the initial relaxation technique that you are currently practicing several times a day outside of the office.

Relaxation Training

Now you will repeat the 11-muscle-group relaxation exercise and record your level of relaxation on a scale of 0 to 10 (see chapter 4 for the relaxation script). You need to practice this skill regularly so that you can ready yourself for the exposure-based part of this treatment, as discussed briefly earlier. Once you have mastered the exercise, you will be able to begin to think about the situations that ordinarily provoke anxiety. You will feel less arousal, however, when using relaxation. Your goal is to be able to relax more quickly and more deeply each time you perform the exercise. This will be accomplished by using progressively shorter relaxation techniques in later sessions.

Homework

- ✎ Begin reading your MVA aloud on a daily basis, and record the number of times you read it each day in your homework diary.

- ✎ Continue practicing the 11-muscle-group relaxation technique, and record your level of relaxation on a 0- to 10-point scale using the relaxation rating scale.

Chapter 6

Session 3

Overview

In this session, you will begin to use coping statements daily. Put yourself in situations in which this self-talk can be used.

You'll begin to list the distressing travel situations or events related to the MVA and rate them using the Subjective Units of Discomfort Scale.

During this session, your spouse or partner will join you for a generalized discussion of your symptoms and treatment.

You will also learn the 8-muscle-group relaxation technique.

Goals

- To review your records from the previous week
- To start to use coping self-statements daily
- To learn to face your travel-related fears
- To involve your spouse or partner in the session
- To learn the eight-muscle-group relaxation technique
- To identify exercises for home practice

Records Review

Before we begin the third step, let's review how you've done so far.

How did the reading of the description of your MVA go? Are you finding it somewhat easier to read the description without getting upset? You'll find that, as you continue to read the description, your anxiety will decrease over time.

How about the relaxation exercise? Are you practicing this exercise several times a day outside of the office? Are you beginning to relax more quickly and easily each time?

Coping Self-Statements

Coping self-statements are ways of using internal dialogue to manage potentially provocative situations. There are three ways to use coping self-statements.

Preparing for Stressful Situations

In many situations, we can predict when stress and anxiety will occur. The time of day, the type of traffic that you will encounter, and the situations that you will encounter often can be predicted. Other situations, such as meeting with a lawyer, physician, or relative, may not even be related to driving, but may be stressful. These are all situations in which coping statements can be utilized.

Suddenly Finding Yourself in a Stressful Travel Situation

Another possibility would be to suddenly find yourself in a stressful situation that you had not prepared for. In this case, you need to endure the situation and get through it. Several examples come to mind. The roads were fine when you left, but the weather changed suddenly. Traffic was light, and then suddenly, you found yourself surrounded by trucks. How can you cope with these situations? Again, coping self-statements can be utilized in a way that will help you to minimize your anxiety and fearful reactions and enable you to better endure these situations and lessen any negative reaction.

Dealing With the Aftermath of a Stressful Situation

Coping self-statements also can be used once the stressful situation is over. How you think about or size up the situation is greatly affected by how you remember and understand what took place (see the Positive Coping Self-Statements form on page 48).

Example of Using Coping Self-Statements

The story of Cheryl provides an example of how to use coping self-statements to prepare for stressful events.

Case Study: Cheryl

Cheryl had trouble when she passed the scene of her MVA; unfortunately, it was necessary for her to pass the accident site (an intersection) frequently because of the way the streets ran in her small town. Each time she began to drive past the site, she knew ahead of time that it would be upsetting and that she would have a terrible time and would not want to go, that she'd want to avoid the trip altogether. Then she began to think about the situation differently. She knew that the accident scene was a relatively quiet road, with little traffic. She knew that she could handle driving past she scene because she had already done it on several occasions. She also learned that her worrying led to worsening of her anxiety. She further recognized that she had been through many difficult situations in her life, and that driving past this accident site was certainly something that she could manage.

She began to use the relaxation exercise before she got into her car, taking a deep breath and recalling the relaxation sensations. She knew that she could put her mind to this task. She would stay in her lane, focus on the car in front of her, and maintain a safe and reasonable distance. She reminded herself that she would be able to pass the MVA scene in a matter of just a few seconds.

We recognize that deliberately using coping self-statements will feel artificial to some people. You may think, "These aren't my real thoughts." This statement is partially true and partially false. We believe that it is important to control your thoughts and the messages you give yourself in this useful, adaptive fashion. They are, in fact, your thoughts, and you can control them. The more you use coping self-statements and rational thoughts, the more natural they will feel.

Difficulty Returning to Driving

After an MVA, it is very normal to have difficulty returning to driving. At first, it is often easier just to think about the situations that can occur when you are in a car and then to rate how distressing those thoughts are. For

Positive Coping Self-Statements

Instructions

Following are some sample statements that you can say to yourself in place of negative "automatic" thoughts that may occur in stressful situations. You can photocopy this page and keep it with you as a reminder, or you can put a copy in a prominent place until you become familiar with the technique. If you don't find these coping self-statements helpful, there is space on the sheet to add your own. Feel free to try different statements in different situations until you find some that work.

1. *In preparation for stressful situations that you can predict will occur, try the following:*
    - (a) What is the specific thing I have to do?
    - (b) What plan can I develop for dealing with this?
    - (c) This situation is not impossible. I can handle it.
    - (d) Don't worry. Worrying isn't going to help anyway.
    - (e) I have a great many resources. I can put them to use in this situation.
    - (f) What am I scared of?
    - (g) I have a lot of support from people who deal with this problem all the time.
    - (h) _____
    - (i) _____

2. *During the course of a stressful situation, try the following (confrontation and coping):*
    - (a) I can manage this situation, if I just take it one step at a time.
    - (b) I've gotten through tougher situations than this before. This will not overwhelm me. It just feels that way at times.
    - (c) I can see this situation as a challenge or an opportunity to improve, rather than as an annoyance or a burden.
    - (d) These are the specific things I need to do to get through the situation (then list the steps).
    - (e) Relax. Calm down. I'm in control of this. Take a slow, deep breath.
    - (f) Let's keep focused on the present. What do I have to do?
    - (g) These feelings are a signal to use the coping skills I'm learning. I can expect the fear to increase, but it will not stop or overwhelm me. This feeling will pass; it always has.
    - (h) _____
    - (i) _____

3. *After the situation is over, try the following:*
    - (a) I need to pay attention to what worked.
    - (b) I need to give myself credit for making a good effort and for any improvement, large or small.
    - (c) All things considered, I did a good job.
    - (d) I'm learning how to deal with this situation more effectively. The next time, I'll do even better.
    - (e) I knew I could handle this. It just takes some time, patience, and effort.
    - (f) That wasn't as bad as I expected.
    - (g) I am making progress.
    - (h) _____
    - (i) _____

example, you may be comfortable driving close to home in light traffic. However, you may feel very anxious if you are placed in certain situations, such as driving on a highway in heavy traffic. You may find it especially problematic to drive past the scene of your accident or to see scenes of car accidents on television or in the newspaper. These are situations that many people want to avoid. The natural way to reduce unpleasant feelings is to avoid the things and situations that provoke fear and distress.

Just as we asked you to confront the ideas and memories associated with your MVA in the reading task, we will also be asking you to gradually confront the situations in real life—to expose yourself to fear-provoking situations. The same technique of gradual exposure to memories that provoke fear and anxiety applies to real-life situations.

We would like you to make a list of travel situations that provoke a response that is negative and distressing. Use the Subjective Units of Discomfort Scale (SUDS) of 0 to 100 points, where 0 = no discomfort and 100 = great, almost overwhelming discomfort. We would like you to make a list of 3 to 5 of these events during this session and then add another 7 to 10 during the week before session 4. Some situations should be minimally distressing (e.g., sitting in a car in a parking lot, driving on a quiet street on a Sunday morning). Others may be more distressing. Examples include changes in the density of traffic (e.g., light to heavy) that can occur simply as a result of driving at different times of day or on different type of roads (e.g., country road to highway). A more distressing situation might be driving by the scene of your accident. Ideally, your list should include a range of distressing situations or events. What we suggest at this time is that you make the list fairly comprehensive, including more than 10 items. A list of typically avoided situations is provided here to help you think of areas that might be important for you.

Situations That Are Typically Avoided by Motor Vehicle Accident Survivors

- Driving past the scene of the accident
- Riding as a passenger in a car
- Seeing an MVA on television or in a movie
- Seeing a photograph of an accident in the newspaper

- Hearing an accident described on television
- Having an acquaintance ask about your MVA or ask how you've been doing since the accident
- Participating in a deposition related to your MVA
- Driving on a highway
- Driving in congested areas
- Driving in bad weather or difficult conditions (e.g., snow, darkness, rain)
- Riding in the back seat of a car

Travel Hierarchy

An example of a completed travel hierarchy showing situations arranged from "easiest" to "hardest," according to their SUDS ratings, can be found on page 51. On page 52 you will find a blank travel hierarchy form that you can use.

Introduction to Exposure

Over the next few weeks, you will be asked to confront a number of situations that are difficult and are likely to cause a fair degree of discomfort. As you begin the task of confronting these situations, it is very important for you to be as prepared as possible to succeed.

Before the next session, you should have a number of situations listed on your travel hierarchy. Also, you should have rated the degree of discomfort that you believe those situations will create (their SUDS rating). The next steps are as follows:

- List additional distressing scenes or situations (8–12, if possible).
- Rate each scene on the 0- to 100-point rating scale (0 = no discomfort, 100 = worst imaginable discomfort).
- There should be a good range of scores, ranging from mild discomfort to great discomfort.

Sample Completed Travel Hierarchy

SUDS Rating

10	1.	Imagine driving around the block
30–35	2.	Watch an MVA on television
40	3.	Sit in the car in the driveway
60	4.	Drive around a familiar neighborhood
70	5.	Drive on city streets with moderate traffic
90	6.	Drive on a highway
100	7.	Drive past the MVA scene
	8.	
	9.	
	10.	
	11.	
	12.	

0 = No discomfort
100 = Great discomfort

- Gradually begin to expose yourself to each scene. This means that you should attempt to place yourself in each situation, beginning with the easiest. Once you have completed a task with little or no discomfort, proceed to the next.

You will be confronting these tasks by using the relaxation skill that you are learning (first, try to relax as much as possible before you attempt the task). Then, as in the situation, you will use relaxation to help manage any discomfort or anxiety that arises.

You will want to use imaginal exposure first. With this technique, before you actually attempt any task, you first imagine the event, imagine your reaction, and imagine how you want to deal with the situation when you face it. Practice success. Use the relaxation and coping statements to plan a way to succeed.

Blank Travel Hierarchy

SUDS Rating

_____	1. _____
_____	2. _____
_____	3. _____
_____	4. _____
_____	5. _____
_____	6. _____
_____	7. _____
_____	8. _____
_____	9. _____
_____	10. _____
_____	11. _____
_____	12. _____
_____	13. _____
_____	14. _____
_____	15. _____

0 = No discomfort
100 = Great discomfort

Bringing Your Spouse or Partner to the Session

At this point, your therapist will ask your spouse or partner to join the session.

There are several reasons why the therapist may ask to meet with him or her, including:

1. Your spouse or partner may be confused and concerned about how you're feeling and why you're feeling that way. It's important for your spouse or partner to recognize that you are having an understandable and common problem and that you've had a normal reaction to an abnormal event (trauma).

2. Sometimes, without meaning to, your spouse or partner may make you feel worse. He or she may try to force you to do something that makes you feel worse, such as driving in difficult circumstances. Your spouse or partner may even say mean things in an effort to make things the way they were before the accident. Such efforts can add a great deal of strain to the relationship.

3. Your spouse or partner may play an important role in which he or she can support you while you go through treatment. Sometimes, this means that your spouse or partner will take over a number of your duties and unintentionally help you to avoid situations that you ultimately need to face. However, deciding when and how to face them should be approached in a therapeutic way, as opposed to a way that can actually add to the amount of anxiety you feel and perpetuate the problem. The goal of this meeting is to help your spouse or partner to better understand how and when to help you, as someone who cares about you. This will also help them avoid seeing themselves or acting as though they were another therapist.

Many people do not easily understand the reactions you are going through. The therapist will try to increase that understanding and help your home situation, which can have a dramatic impact on how you're feeling and how the problems will be addressed in the weeks to come.

8-Muscle-Group Relaxation Training

At this point, your spouse or partner will leave the session so that you are able to learn this new, shorter relaxation exercise.

Muscle Groups Used for the 8-Muscle-Group Relaxation Exercise

- Both arms
- Both legs and hips
- Abdomen
- Chest
- Shoulders
- Neck
- Eyes and forehead
- Lower face

8-Muscle-Group Relaxation Exercise Script

To begin this exercise, I'd like you make yourself comfortable. In a moment, I'll ask you to close your eyes and just listen to my voice. Then, just let whatever happens happen, without any effort or strain. Just let go. You can't force relaxation, but you can set the stage for it to occur.

Begin now by closing your eyes and focusing on your breathing. Breathe in and out. Find a rhythm that's right for you. Again, you'll notice that, as you relax, your breathing will slow down. Just let it happen, and store away that feeling, if it does occur.

We'll begin the tensing exercise by focusing first on the muscles of your arms, both arms. Start by tensing your hands, your lower arms, and your upper arms. Again, try to hold the tension for about 10 seconds, noticing where the tension is created and really feeling the tightness in your muscles, every fiber. Hold it, being very aware of your fingers, hands, lower arms, and upper arms . . . and then relax. Just let go, and focus on the difference. Contrast how your muscles felt when they were tight and how they feel now. Imagine that the relaxation is spreading up your arm like a wave . . . warm, heavy, quiet, calm. As the wave ebbs, the tension leaves. Store those feelings away, as we move our attention to the lower body . . . the legs and hips.

Here, we'll begin by having you tighten your muscles once again, this time focusing on the entire lower body. Your hips and buttocks are tight and hard, and your upper legs, the quads, the hamstrings, all the way down into the lower legs and feet, are tight and hard. You're really feeling the tension. Then relax, focusing again on the change. Really notice how your muscles feel now . . . warm, calm, and comfortable. Notice the change . . . the contrast between how the muscles felt when they were tight and hard and how they feel now, as they grow calm and loose, peaceful . . . comfortable. Just let the feelings of relaxation wash over you like a wave, full and calm, spreading relaxation into your whole lower body, and then washing the tension away . . . quiet, peaceful. Store those differences away, and then deepen your relaxation. Just let go, more . . . and more . . . as your relaxation gets deeper and deeper.

Now our attention moves to the stomach, focusing on the abdomen and lower back. We'll begin by having you tense your muscles as you take a nice, deep breath. First, fill your lungs. Take a nice, deep, full breath. Hold it, and then tense your stomach by pressing it out, distending it, and feeling the tension in your back, sides, and stomach. Hold it, hold it . . . then relax. Just let go. Let the next breath in be a full, slow breath, and as you exhale, feel any tension leave.

Again, you may feel the muscles grow warm and loose as your relaxation deepens and grows. Whatever you feel, store those feelings away as you notice the difference between how the muscles felt when they were tight and how they feel now, as they relax. Now we'll move our attention up to the muscles of the chest and upper back.

Here, we'll start again with a breath. When you're ready, fill your lungs and tighten the muscles in your chest. Imagine that a belt or band has been pulled tight across your chest. Just notice those feelings. Imagine where the tension is and how it feels to let go and relax. Then, breathe in, a fresh, clean, cleansing breath, and as you exhale, think "relax" . . . in . . . out . . . relax . . . calm.

Now, we move our attention up to the muscles of your shoulders. I'd like you to hunch your shoulders up, tightening them, as you push your shoulder up. Feel the tension in your shoulders, on the right, on the left, and in the lower neck . . . feeling the tightness . . . and then relax. Just let go. Focus on the difference. Feel your shoulders sag and grow limp and loose. Store those feelings away. Just allow the muscles to grow calm, quiet, comfortable, and peaceful. We move our attention now to the neck itself.

Now I'd like you to push your head back, into the cushion, if you're using one, and feel the tension. Notice where the tension is created and how it feels. Hold it, not too hard, but hard enough to feel the tightness, and then relax. Just let go. Let your head find a comfortable position, and settle into that spot deeply and fully, as you focus on the difference. Remember how your muscles felt when they were tight. Again, notice how they feel as they relax, becoming more and more calm and quiet. Now, we move our attention up to the muscles of the face.

We'll begin with the muscles of your forehead and eyes. To begin, squint your eyes, closing them firmly, pulling down on your forehead and temples, really focusing on the muscles of your upper face. Notice where tension is held and how it feels, storing that feeling in your mind, and then relax Just let go, and feel the difference. Focus on the change as the muscles grow longer and loosen. Notice how that feels, and focus on those feelings . . . calm, quiet, and peaceful. Just store those feelings away, as we move to the lower face and jaw.

Now, I'd like you to tighten your jaw by clenching your teeth, pulling your lips back, and pressing your tongue into the roof of your mouth. Notice where the tension is held, hold onto those feelings, and then relax. Just let go, all the way. Your jaw just hangs, loose . . . quiet. Focus on the feeling. Remember the feeling from the earlier exercise, and bring that memory now to mind, deeper and deeper, more and more complete.

In your mind, go through your entire body, from head to toe. Focus on each muscle group, deepening the feeling as you think about each muscle . . . your hands, your arms . . . deeper, relaxed.

Legs, hips . . . quiet, calm.

Stomach, lower back . . . relaxed.

Chest . . . quiet, calm, comfortable.

Shoulders, neck . . . peaceful.

Forehead and eyes . . . loose, limp.

Lower face and jaw . . . quiet, deeply relaxed.

Now, I'd like you to focus on your breathing, and for the next five breaths, count each time you inhale, and then think the word "relax" as you exhale.

One. Breathe in, and then relax. Find your rhythm, your cycle.

Two. Relax.

Three. Relax more deeply.

Four. Relax.

Five. Relax, fully, and deeply.

In a moment, it will be time to open your eyes. Again, we'll count backward from three to one. Each time you practice this exercise, you'll gain in skill and your relaxation will grow deeper and last longer and longer, becoming easier and easier to create. But now, we'll start to come back. Three. You're still very deeply relaxed. Two. You're a little more alert, maybe moving around just a bit. One. You're all the way back, alert, yet calm, and very comfortable.

- add right movement to coming out of session

Homework

- Continue reading your MVA description aloud on a daily basis, and record the number of times you read it each day.

- Begin practicing the 8-muscle-group relaxation training exercise several times daily, and record your level of relaxation on a 0- to 10-point scale, using the relaxation rating scale.

- Begin using coping self-statements.

- Continue to work on your travel hierarchy until you have a list of 10 to 15 items.

- Keep records of all of your homework assignments using the homework diary.

Chapter 7

Session 4

Overview

In this session, you will be introduced to cognitive reappraisal.

You will also review the exposure hierarchy that you completed after session 3, and you will work with your therapist to begin in vivo exposure.

You will also learn the briefer 4-muscle-group relaxation technique.

Goals

- To review your records from the previous week
- To learn cognitive reappraisal
- To begin working up the driving hierarchy (using both in vivo and imaginal practice)
- To learn how to use the four-muscle-group relaxation exercise
- To identify exercises for home practice

Records Review

Your therapist will want to review your homework.

Cognitive Reappraisal

Once you understand how coping self-statements can be applied, you are ready to understand how thoughts can affect how you feel and act. Any situation can be viewed from a number of perspectives. It is very common for an MVA survivor to view most situations as more dangerous than they had been before the accident. This pattern of thinking can become so automatic that you don't even realize that you are doing it. This shift in perception is normal, but that does not mean that your thoughts are accurate. As you become more and more aware of your thoughts, you will see that the way you think about a situation can have a significant effect on what you experience and how you act.

In the 1950s, Albert Ellis, a psychologist, described a very direct model for breaking down thoughts and explaining how our thoughts affect our subsequent feelings and actions. It's easy to think that the situation that you are in provokes your reaction. For example, when you drive past your accident site, you become upset. Albert Ellis showed us very clearly that it is not the "activating" event (e.g., driving past the accident site) that produces distress; rather, it is how we think about the accident site that is important. Many people drive past the same site and don't get upset. You used to drive past that same place without getting upset. Something changed. Ellis would argue that what changed is how you have begun to think about the site since you've had your accident. He then goes on to show a way to attack and change this pattern of thinking, once you understand how your thoughts became distorted or altered.

Ellis begins to explain how this works with a very simple A-B-C-D model.

A-B-C-D Model of Cognitive Reappraisal

The A-B-C-D model depicts the sequence of events that occur when you are trying to change an overly negative interpretation of a situation. The *activating event* (A) is what actually happened during the stressful situation. The *belief* (B) that you have about the situation is how you interpreted it. The *consequence* (C) includes how you felt and how you acted in the situation. Finally, the active part of cognitive reappraisal is how you *dispute* (D), or reevaluate, your "automatic" negative appraisal, with the goal of replacing those maladaptive beliefs and perceptions with more realistic and accurate ones.

Here is an outline of the cognitive reappraisal model:

A = Activating event (What happened?)

B = Belief (What were you thinking when it happened?)

C = Consequence (How did you feel and what did you do in the situation?)

D = Dispute (How might you challenge your overly negative beliefs?)

We know that it takes some time to learn about our thoughts and how they can affect our feelings and behaviors. It is important, however, that you begin to understand that the way you think about something can have a dramatic effect on how you will feel and what you will be able to do. We often attribute anxiety to an external event (e.g., passing the scene of the accident while riding as a passenger, and hearing the screech of brakes). However, the A-B-C-D model begins the process of showing how it is actually our thoughts ("I can't stand seeing the place where my accident occurred. You shouldn't drive that way; it's awful not to have control when in a car. See, another accident almost happened! I told you it's not safe on the road.") that lead to anxiety, fear, or tension. Some fallacies, or distortions of thinking, can be summarized as a tendency to catastrophize an event and think about the "what if's" that could spell disaster. It doesn't matter that the disaster didn't occur; the fact that it might occur becomes the focus of your reaction. This tendency to overemphasize danger and minimize safety after a car crash is common, and it illustrates how a thought can lead to an undesirable reaction. The same is true of the statement that the squeal of brakes proves that the roads are unsafe. Other possibilities for this sound include a noisy brake pad and a driver stopping in plenty of time, but overreacting. Another example of distorted thinking is seeing the driver of a car as unsafe because you're not driving, even when the driver has a very safe driving record. The thoughts lead to the reaction. Over the next few weeks, try to see if you can identify any thoughts that might be similar to one of the situations discussed earlier or listed as a common problem area. Then see if you can dispute the thought by asking yourself to provide proof of its accuracy or asking yourself if there might be other, more realistic ways to see the same events. Where is the proof that people should drive the way you think they should? It's true that it might be better if more people drove more slowly and maintained more distance between vehicles, for example, but your opinion is unlikely to change the reality of how people drive.

Common Cognitive Distortions After a Motor Vehicle Accident

- Overprediction of your own fear when in a car
- Overprediction of the potential danger when in a car
- Heightened attention to potential threats while driving
- Decreased attention to factors related to your safety while in a car
- Not acknowledging your own driving skills
- Not acknowledging the competency of other drivers
- Catastrophizing the outcome of a future MVA (if it were to happen)
- Not acknowledging your own ability to cope and deal with a future MVA or injury

Test Exercise for Cognitive Reappraisal

Applying the A-B-C-D Model of Cognitive Reappraisal to life-situations needs practice. The A-B-C-D Model is a very useful tool, so any time you spend really learning and "digesting" the steps will be rewarding. On pages 64–65 you will find a Test Exercise for Cognitive Reappraisal. This exercise gives a chance to try out your new skills on some driving situations. Please complete this exercise at home during the coming week, and bring the completed test exercise with you to your next session, when your therapist will go over each of your answers with you. Before you start the exercise, take the time to re-read and familiarize yourself with the sections in your workbook that discuss the A-B-C-D Model of Cognitive Reappraisal and the Common Cognitive Distortions After a MVA.

Travel Hierarchy

You should have completed your travel hierarchy record form by this session, and now you will start to take on the less stressful situations on your list until you can master them. Mastering your fears requires you to place yourself in the situations and deal with them using the skills and tools you are learning in treatment. The first skill you have learned is relaxation. We would like you to use relaxation to achieve a relaxed state, and then to imagine going through scene that is lowest on your hierarchy. This is called "imaginal exposure." As you imagine yourself driving or riding in the situation that you have described, try to maintain a sense of relaxation as best you can, repeating this exercise over and over again, until there is a lessening of the response.

The next step is to do what is called "in vivo exposure," which means placing yourself in real-life situations rather than using your imagination. This would mean actually doing the tasks at the lower end of the avoidance hierarchy and exposing yourself to the situations gradually, until you can face them without much distress. Slowly, work your way up the hierarchy, until you can face the most fearful situations on your list.

Instructions for Exposure

Referring to your completed Travel Hierarchy form, taking the following steps:

- List additional distressing scenes or situations (8–12, if possible).

- Rate each scene on the 0- to 100-point rating scale (0 = no discomfort, 100 = worst imaginable discomfort).

- There should be a good range of scores, ranging from mild discomfort to great discomfort.

- Begin to expose yourself to the lower-rated scenes. This means that you should attempt to place yourself in each situation, beginning with the easiest. Once you have completed a task with little or no discomfort, slowly proceed to the next.

You will confront these tasks by using the relaxation skill that you are learning (first, try to relax as much as possible before you attempt the task). Then, as in the situation, use relaxation to help manage any discomfort or anxiety that arises. The second tool that you are learning to use is cognitive coping skills. In addition to using coping statements, this means trying to understand how your thoughts are impacting (either negatively of positively) how your feelings are created. (Refer back to the A-B-C-D Model of Cognitive Reappraisal on pages 60–62 as often as you need to). Use these techniques to plan for the event, to talk your way through it, and to evaluate your effort afterward.

Test Exercise for Cognitive Reappraisal

We have now set up a series of situations. We would like you to try to apply either coping self-statements or the A-B-C-D model to see how well you have learned them. Answers are provided at the end of chapter 8.

John was driving to the store when suddenly the car in front of him cut him off. John became angry. He started yelling, "How dare you! You're supposed to signal before you change lanes! You could have killed me!"

What possible distortions did John make in his appraisal of the scene? How could he dispute these distortions? Use the A-B-C-D model:

A = Activating event: _____

B = Belief: _____

C = Consequence: _____

D = Dispute: _____

Mary was riding in the car with her husband Pete. Pete has always been a good driver. He's never been in an accident. However, since her accident, Mary now finds Pete is just too aggressive. He drives too fast and gets too close to the cars in front of them. Several times during each ride she'll have to tell Pete to slow down, that he's too close, and that he'd be in a terrible accident if the other driver stopped without warning.

What is Mary telling herself that is raising her level of concern? How can she dispute these ideas?

A = Activating event: _____

B = Belief: _____

C = Consequence: _____

D = Dispute: _____

Sally has had several panic attacks and now is worried that one would come when driving. If she were to have a panic attack while driving, she knew it would lead to an accident and probably kill her.
   Identify the A-B-C's and Dispute:

A = Activating event: _____

B = Belief: _____

C = Consequence: _____

D = Dispute: _____

Cheryl didn't tell her husband, but she started worrying about getting into another accident. The drivers on the road just seemed out of control. It was just a matter of time before one hit her again. The next accident, she knew, would be fatal. How could she leave the house?
   Identify the A-B-C's and Dispute:

A = Activating event: _____

B = Belief: _____

C = Consequence: _____

D = Dispute: _____

Answers to the questions above can be found at the end of chapter 8.

Keep track on your homework sheet of what happens as you tackle each new task on your Travel Hierarchy. If you proceed too quickly through the tasks, you might become anxious or panicky. It is important that you stop immediately if your anxiety feels unmanageable. If that happens, please stop the task, use a relaxation exercise, and try to understand what happened and why. Did your thoughts contribute to the increase in anxiety? Were there physical feelings that you didn't manage? Try to learn as much as possible from the experience so that something of worth will come from it, and it will become less likely to increase the experience of anxiety in the future. Then go back to an easier task on the hierarchy list, and perform it repeatedly until you can complete it easily and without discomfort. Then and only then, try to increase the level of difficulty of the task that you are approaching.

4-Muscle-Group Relaxation Exercise

The purpose of this exercise is to begin to reduce the number of muscle groups required to achieve a state of deep relaxation, as well as to shorten the time needed to achieve a relaxed state so that this tool may be applied to stressful situations. This briefer relaxation technique includes the following four muscle groups:

- Both arms together
- Chest and stomach, using a deep breath
- Neck and shoulders
- Face and eyes

Remember, relaxation is a learned skill. It will come only with regular practice.

4-Muscle-Group Relaxation Script

Start by finding a comfortable position. Settle down, close your eyes, and take a breath. Fill your lungs with fresh, clean air, and when you're ready, exhale. Try to find a rhythm to your breathing that is comfortable for you. Rising and falling, very comfortable. Begin to think of the word "relax" every time you exhale, and feel the relaxation beginning to spread throughout your body.

Begin the exercise by starting to focus on your hands and arms on both the right and left sides. I would like you to start by making a fist, first with your right hand and then with your left hand, tensing both arms. Feel the tension across your fingers, thumb, wrist, and forearm. Feel the tension all the way up both arms, on the right and left sides. Hold that tension. Be very aware of that tension . . . holding it, noticing it . . . and notice where all the tightness is held. Then relax. Focus on the difference. Focus on the difference between where you felt the tension and how the relaxation is growing.

Imagine the relaxation feeling as if a wave has just washed up your arm, bringing a warm and comfortable sensation wherever it touches, and as it ebbs away, taking all of the tension with it. Some people find that, when the relaxation grows deep, the arm feels warm and heavy. Other people feel that it grows light as the tension leaves. Whatever it feels like for you, store away those feelings. Now we'll move our attention down to the muscles in the lower body.

The next step is to tense the muscles in your legs, feet, hips, and buttocks all at once. To do this, start by tensing your feet. Curl your toes, and tense your toes, the balls of your feet, and your ankles and calves, right up into your thighs, pressing your legs hard, right into your hips and buttocks, pressing down so that your entire lower body is made hard and firm. Feel the tightness. Be very aware of these sensations. Hold the tightness, notice it, being very aware of where all of the tightness is held, and then relax. Just let it go. As you let it go, let all of the tension leave. Let the relaxation enter. Again, focus on the difference. Feel the relaxation washing over you, like a warm, comfortable wave, bringing deep, full relaxation, and as it ebbs away, taking all of the tension with it. You're feeling calm, quiet, and peaceful. Allow those feelings to deepen and grow. With the next few breaths, every time you exhale, feel the relaxation spreading down, deeper and deeper, as you become more relaxed with every breath.

Now, move your attention up to the muscles in your stomach and chest. You are going to create tension a little differently here. Start with a good, deep breath, and then tighten the muscles, hold your breath, and relax as you exhale. Whenever you're ready, take a good, deep breath, filling your lungs. As you fill your lungs, hold the tightness. Feel the tightness like a band or belt placed around your chest, and hold the tight feeling in your stomach. Tense the muscles in your abdomen, being very aware of all of the tension there. Hold the tightness, being very aware of where the tautness is held, and whenever you are ready, slowly exhale. Imagine the next breath in as a fresh, clean cleansing breath. As you exhale, just imagine all of the tightness leaving. Also, notice that when you fill your lungs, your stomach rises with your chest. As you exhale, feel your stomach sink with your chest.

Focus on the middle of your trunk. You're breathing from your diaphragm, as your chest and stomach rise as one and empty as one. Relax those muscles all the way, sink deeply into the cushion, and let all of the tension leave. Let the relaxation grow deeper and deeper as you feel more and more relaxed. We will come back to this breathing in just a few moments. It's very important that you learn to relax your chest and stomach by controlling your breathing.

Now we will move to the muscles in your shoulders, neck, face, and scalp. Start by pressing your head back, and then raise your shoulders, press your forehead down, squint your eyes, and clench your jaw, so that all of the muscles in this area are hard and firm. Feel the tightness, being aware of the sensations, and then relax. Just let it go. As you let all of the tension leave, let your shoulders sag, as you feel calm and quiet. Your forehead grows smooth as the muscles grow longer and become less constricted. You may feel tingling and warmth in the muscles. Whatever you feel, just focus on those sensations, deepen them, and let them grow, as your relaxation grows deeper and deeper.

We have gone through all of the muscles once, and we will go through them a second time. This time, don't tighten the muscles. Just focus on them, trying to relax them just a little bit. Forehead, eyes, relaxed and calm. Lower face and jaw, loose, comfortable. Your neck and shoulders are growing relaxed and heavy, peaceful, and quiet. Your chest and upper back are relaxed, and your breathing is full and calm. Every time you exhale, just imagine the relaxation spreading throughout your body. Just feel your chest and stomach rising and falling, feeling calmer and calmer with every breath. Your hips and upper legs are relaxed and heavy, and your lower legs and feet are relaxed. All of the tension is draining down and out, as your relaxation deepens and grows. Your arms, down your upper arms, down your lower arms, and out your hands and fingers. Relaxed and calm.

In your mind, go through your body, from head to toe. Wherever you feel tension, try to release it, as your relaxation becomes even deeper and you feel calmer and quieter, more and more relaxed. Focus on your breathing, rising and falling, filling your lungs very naturally and comfortably. As you relax, feel yourself sinking into the cushions, feeling very, very calm and very, very peaceful.

Now imagine yourself in a very relaxing place. As completely and vividly as you can, I would like you to create that place. Imagine yourself there now, in a warm, comfortable, quiet place. Feel the sun, see the color of the sky, see the clouds or birds, see the water, smell the water, and hear whether it's waves or a stream. You're lying on a beach. Feel the warmth and grit of the sand beneath you. You're lying on grass. Feel the coolness of it. Whatever is there, just create it vividly, fully, with your mind, and enjoy the feelings you are experiencing. Find a spot or place that is memorable, one that is easy to recall. Every time you do the relaxation exercise, as you become deeply relaxed, I would like you to think of this place, this image, or this scene. Imagine how deeply relaxed you would be if you were there. Remember those feelings, remember the contrast between how you felt when your muscles were tight and how you feel when you are fully relaxed. Now it's time to come back, as I count backward from three to one. When I get to one, slowly open your eyes, coming all the way back, but continue to remember deep and full relaxation. Three. You're starting to come out. You're still very, very comfortable. Two. You're a little more alert, perhaps moving around just a bit. One. You're all the way back. Slowly open your eyes, feeling alert, calm, and quiet.

Homework

- Continue reading your MVA description aloud on a daily basis, and record the number of times you read it each day.

- In consultation with your therapist, begin exposure exercises, first using imaginal exposure and then moving on to in vivo exposure.

- Practice cognitive reappraisal skills and complete the Test Exercise for Cognitive Reappraisal (be sure to bring the completed exercise with you to your next session).

- Begin practicing the 4-muscle-group relaxation technique, and record your level of relaxation using the 11-point relaxation rating scale.

- Keep records of all of your homework assignments using the homework diary.

Chapter 8   *Session 5*

Overview

In this session, you will again review all of your homework assignments.

Most of this session will be spent reviewing your travel hierarchy and evaluating your exposure progress.

You will also learn the relaxation-by-recall technique.

Goals

- To review your records from the previous week
- To continue exposing yourself to the feared situations listed on your travel hierarchy (using both in vivo and imaginal practice)
- To review self-talk and how it can be changed to help you cope with the situations on the hierarchy
- To learn the relaxation-by-recall technique
- To identify exercises for home practice

Records Review

At this point, you may be bored with reading your MVA description aloud several times per day. If this is the case, your therapist will instruct you to read it only once per day for the remainder of your treatment. If the MVA is still causing you some distress, stay with it, reading it aloud 3 or 4 times each day, and continue to work on this with your therapist.

Your therapist will also review with you your answers to the Test Exercise for Cognitive Reappraisal (from pages 64–65) that you worked on during the past week. Your therapist will make sure that you feel confident in applying each step of the A-B-C-D Method. For your future use and reference, we have provided an answer sheet that you will find at the very end of this chapter (page 75).

Travel Hierarchy Review

During this part of the session, your therapist will review your progress, moving up the travel hierarchy that you created in session 3.

It is very important that you understand that treatment should take place only in what are called "graduated steps." This means that you should start small and build with regular progression, rather than trying to leap all the way to the worst, most distressing situation listed on your hierarchy.

However, it's not always possible to move in slow, graduated steps. Although not ideal, this situation has been addressed in our clinic-based treatments. Some of our patients have, in fact, taken vacations during the middle of treatment that required extensive driving. They were able to use the imaginal and behavioral techniques to prepare themselves for the in vivo exposure. By this, we mean that they would imagine themselves on the trip, use relaxation to control their responses, imagine the situations that would cause anxiety, and then practice as well as they could before the trip. Then they went on their trip. Although this approach is not successful for everyone, a good number of people have reported to us very significant progress as a result of having this unavoidable protracted period in the automobile. However, in each case, the patient prepared for the trip in this fashion. Notice that the easier, less stressful events are practiced first; these situations are used to gain success for later items.

Even as you achieve success along the hierarchy, it is important to understand that each of the steps listed earlier requires attention. Every thought or situation that has led to a reaction must be dealt with until the reaction is minimized. It is also common for new situations and thoughts to come to mind as you practice these techniques. These situations should be added to the list, placed within the hierarchy, and then dealt with in a similar fashion.

In an effort to avoid certain situations, you may put off doing what you promised yourself you would do to help yourself, or you may not stay in an uncomfortable situation as long as necessary to benefit from the exposure. Again, we urge you to try to maintain the exposure as long as you can, until your reaction becomes minimal; at times, you may even be bored. We have had certain patients drive on a highway from exit to exit, 20 to 30 times, until they say that it is just so boring that they cannot do the task any longer. This is much preferred to saying that they cannot do the task because it is causing so much anxiety. A reaction of boredom means that the physiological reaction that is part of PTSD has been diminished and put to rest. This is one of our goals for you.

Relaxation-by-Recall

First, you will perform a 4-muscle-group relaxation exercise. Once you are comfortably relaxed, you will go through each muscle group mentally. Try to recall how each group of muscles feels when it is deeply relaxed. Try to have this become a true muscle memory. Recall the feelings associated with deep relaxation for the lower body (feet, legs, and hips), the trunk (stomach, lower back, chest, and upper back), both arms and hands, and the shoulders and face.

If you're able to recall these feelings of relaxation without having to tense the muscles, but just by using recall, congratulations! You have a new tool to use. If you were "pretty successful," continue to supplement relaxation-by-recall with the four-muscle-group relaxation exercise until you can obtain similar feelings with recall alone. If you weren't able to produce a feeling of deep relaxation by recall alone, don't worry. Keep practicing the earlier exercises, and when you feel ready, try again.

Midtreatment Reassessment

About this time, you and your therapist will want to know how you're doing. One of the best ways to do this is to repeat the questionnaires that you completed earlier. Blank copies of the PCL, CES-D, and TAQ can be found in the next chapter (chapter 9). Be sure to fill them out and bring them to the next session (session 6).

Homework

- Continue reading your MVA description aloud on a daily basis, and record the number of times you read it each day. At this point, you may decrease the number of times you read the description to once per day, if you no longer feel much distress when you read it.

- Continue your exposure exercises.

- Remember to use coping self-statements.

- Begin to use the relaxation-by-recall technique, and record your level of relaxation on a 11-point scale using the relaxation rating scale.

- Complete the midtreatment reassessment, and bring your completed PCL, CES-D, and TAQ forms to the next session.

- Keep records of all of your homework assignments using the homework diary.

Answers to Cognitive Reappraisal Test Exercise

John
- A = *Activating Event:* Car cut him off
- B = *Belief:* "You don't act like I want you to! You should follow the rules!"
- C = *Consequence:* Anger and upset
- D = *Dispute:* Who says the world will follow the rules? Does everyone follow the rules? I don't think so. Do you need to get upset at everyone? Were you in that much danger? You saw it coming, you did avoid them.

Mary
- A = Husband drives too fast
- B = It's dangerous, we can have a terrible accident.
- C = Anxiousness
- D = I'm magnifying the danger and forgetting what a good driver Pete has been.

Sally
- A = Panic attack, worry of panic attacks
- B = Next panic attack will lead to an accident and probably kill her.
- C = Worry, anxiety, and fear
- D = Even if you panic, how do you know the next one will kill you? You could pull over and deal with it. You are learning skills to control panic, use them. The worry heightens the anxiety.

Cheryl
- A = Other drivers are too dangerous
- B = If I leave the house, its just a matter of time until I get in an accident that will be fatal
- C = Worry and fear
- D = You're reading the future. You don't know if any of those thoughts are true. You are magnifying the danger and minimizing your own skills and statistics regarding fatalities.

Chapter 9 — Midtreatment Reassessment

Goal

- To use assessment instruments again to determine whether you are making progress

Checking Your Progress

By this point, you've done a lot of work, and we hope that you're feeling better. An important part of any treatment is the ability to see how well you're doing. The assessment instruments that you answered at the start of treatment allow us to determine your progress easily. In this chapter, we provide another copy of the questionnaires that you completed at that time. After you complete them, you can go back and compare your earlier answers with your answers on the questionnaires that you complete now.

Posttraumatic Stress Disorder

First, let's check the symptoms of PTSD that you may be experiencing. A copy of the PCL is provided for this purpose (page 79). You can do this reassessment at any point in your treatment. The timing of the reassessment will be determined by you and your therapist. Some people prefer to take a measure somewhere in the middle of treatment. This helps them to focus on what remains to be done and where to put their greatest effort. It also can help people to decide whether they are making progress.

To complete the PCL, answer the questions in terms of how you've been feeling over the past week. Total your answers, and then compare the results with your initial test. How did you do? If you're making progress, great! The work you've been doing is paying off. If you are not making as much progress as you'd hoped, are you making some progress? Do you think you'll make more progress if you stick with the program a while longer?

Remember, the PCL (Weathers, Litz, Herman, Huska, & Keane, 1993) is a 17-item questionnaire that asks you to rate the severity of each of the 17 symptoms of PTSD from 1 (not at all) to 5 (extremely). The maximum score is 85. We have found that a score of 44 or higher has great predictive capability for identifying PTSD in people who have had an MVA.

Depression

Now it's time to see how your mood has changed. Once again, we've provided you with a copy of the CES-D. Answer the questions in terms of how you've felt over the past week (page 80). Then, look back on your earlier questionnaire and see how you did. Are you making progress? Is your mood improving? Again, depending on your response, you'll need to decide what the next step should be.

Travel Anxiety

The last area to look at is your fear and anxiety related to travel (page 81). Unlike the other questionnaires, this questionnaire doesn't have a set of numbers for easy comparison, but you can certainly look back at how you answered the TAQ before. Is your anxiety getting better? We hope that the exposure exercises, the driving practice, the cognitive techniques, and the relaxation techniques have begun to make a difference.

Summary

The goal of this reassessment is to help you to see the progress that you are making and realize how far you've come. The questionnaires allow you to measure the changes in anxiety (PTSD), mood (depression), and driving behaviors (travel anxiety). The goal is for you to get better. This information can help you to target any remaining difficulties and help you to decide what you need to do to overcome them.

Current Posttraumatic Stress Disorder Checklist (PCL)

Name: _____ Date: _____

Instructions: Following is a list of problems and complaints that people sometimes have in response to stressful life experiences (i.e., **your most distressing MVA**). Please read each one carefully, then circle one of the numbers to the right to indicate how much you have been bothered by that problem and your most distressing MVA *in the past week.*

	Not at All	A Little Bit	Moderately	Quite a Bit	Extremely
1. Repeated, disturbing memories, thoughts, or images of the stressful experience?	1	2	3	4	5
2. Repeated, disturbing dreams of the stressful experience?	1	2	3	4	5
3. Suddenly acting or feeling as if the stressful experience were happening again (as if you were reliving it)?	1	2	3	4	5
4. Feeling very upset when something reminded you of the stressful experience?	1	2	3	4	5
5. Having a physical reaction (e.g., heart pounding, trouble breathing, sweating) when something reminded you of the stressful experience?	1	2	3	4	5
6. Avoiding thinking about or talking about your stressful experience or avoiding having feelings related to it?	1	2	3	4	5
7. Avoiding activities or situations because they reminded you of your stressful experience?	1	2	3	4	5
8. Trouble remembering important parts of the stressful experience?	1	2	3	4	5
9. Loss of interest in activities that you used to enjoy?	1	2	3	4	5
10. Feeling distant or cut off from others?	1	2	3	4	5
11. Feeling emotionally numb or being unable to have loving feelings for those close to you?	1	2	3	4	5
12. Feeling as if your future somehow will be cut short?	1	2	3	4	5
13. Trouble falling or staying asleep?	1	2	3	4	5
14. Feeling irritable or having angry outbursts?	1	2	3	4	5
15. Having difficulty concentrating?	1	2	3	4	5
16. Being "super-alert," watchful, or on guard?	1	2	3	4	5
17. Feeling jumpy or easily startled?	1	2	3	4	5
Total					

Current Center for Epidemiologic Studies–Depression (CES-D)

Name: _____ Date: _____

For each statement, please circle the number that best describes how often you have felt or behaved this way during the **past week**.

	Rarely or None of the Time	Some or a Little of the Time	Occasionally or a Moderate Amount of the Time	Most or All of the Time
I was bothered by things that usually don't bother me	0	1	2	3
I did not feel like eating; my appetite was poor	0	1	2	3
I felt like I could not shake off the blues, even with help from my family or friends	0	1	2	3
I felt like I was just as good as other people	0	1	2	3
I had trouble keeping my mind on what I was doing	0	1	2	3
I felt depressed	0	1	2	3
I felt that everything I did was an effort	0	1	2	3
I felt hopeful about the future	0	1	2	3
I thought my life had been a failure	0	1	2	3
I felt fearful	0	1	2	3
My sleep was restless	0	1	2	3
I was happy	0	1	2	3
I talked less than usual	0	1	2	3
I felt lonely	0	1	2	3
People were unfriendly	0	1	2	3
I enjoyed life	0	1	2	3
I had crying spells	0	1	2	3
I felt sad	0	1	2	3
I felt like people disliked me	0	1	2	3
I could not get "going"*	0	1	2	3
I had thoughts about my death	0	1	2	3
I thought about harming myself	0	1	2	3
Sum of scores				
Total score =				

*Stop scoring after this item.

Travel Anxiety Questionnaire (TAQ)

Name: _____   Date: _____

1. Are you driving at the **present** time? (Circle one)
   1. Yes   Go to question 3
   2. No   Continue to question 2

2. If you are *not* driving presently, why not?
   (Check *all* that apply)
   - ☐ Driving makes me anxious
   - ☐ Physically unable
   - ☐ No car
   - ☐ No license
   - ☐ None of the above

3. Following are eight driving situations. Use the two scales below to **rate how anxious** you are about each situation currently, as well as **how much you avoid** each of these situations **currently.** If the situation does not apply to you, please circle "NA" next to the situation.

   Anxiety rating scale

0	1	2	3	4
No anxiety	Very little anxiety	Some anxiety	Moderate anxiety	Severe anxiety

   Avoidance rating scale

0	1	2	3	4
None of the time	Less than half of the time	About half of the time	More than half of the time	All of the time

	Anxiety rating	Avoidance rating	
Driving at night	_____	_____	NA
Driving in snow	_____	_____	NA
Driving in rain	_____	_____	NA
Highway driving	_____	_____	NA
Driving in heavy traffic	_____	_____	NA
Driving in the location of the MVA	_____	_____	NA
Driving on pleasure trips	_____	_____	NA
Being the passenger	_____	_____	NA

Please circle either yes or no:

4. **Currently,** do you restrict your driving speed?   Yes   No

5. **Currently,** do you drive only to work?   Yes   No

Chapter 10 *Session 6*

Overview

In this session, you will again review all of your homework assignments. You will also review the results of your midtreatment assessment with your therapist.

Most of this session will be spent reviewing your travel hierarchy and evaluating your exposure progress.

You will also learn to use cue-controlled relaxation.

Goals

- To review the records from the previous week
- To continue exposing yourself to feared situations listed on your travel hierarchy (using both in vivo and imaginal practice)
- To learn to use cue-controlled relaxation
- To identify exercises for home practice

Records Review

As discussed in the last chapter, you may be bored with reading your MVA description at this point. If so, discuss this with your therapist. He or she may reduce the number of times that you're required to read it aloud. Although it may seem less important now, reading your MVA description aloud is still a very important part of treatment.

You and your therapist will also review your midtreatment assessment (PCL, CES-D, and TAQ).

Travel Hierarchy Review

The travel hierarchy is your primary focus at this stage of treatment. You should still be working your way up the list, exposing yourself to the feared situations. Again, you may use imaginal exposure for the events on your list that are not easily recreated or that do not occur very often. For all other situations, you should be using in vivo exposure and placing yourself in the actual situation. Use relaxation techniques and cognitive strategies to cope with the anxiety you feel.

By now, you may have a good understanding of in vivo exposure and how to use coping self-talk (chapter 6) and cognitive reappraisal (chapter 7). If so, it is still very important to continue practicing these skills. If you feel as if you are taking a long time to progress through your hierarchy, just keep working at it. Everyone goes at his or her own pace. The important thing is to keep practicing the exposures.

Cue-Controlled Relaxation

The last brief relaxation technique that we'd like to share is cue-controlled relaxation. Once you are using relaxation-by-recall effectively, you can try to produce relaxation by setting up cues in the environment that are associated with relaxation. First, take a deep breath by raising your stomach, and as you exhale, think the word "relax." This should be very familiar to you by now, and at first, you can do it with your eyes closed, and then later, with your eyes open. If you'd like, think of some relaxing imagery to help you relax from head to toe. Once you've done that, your next task is to tie the relaxation to commonly occurring situations in your life. For instance you may find that, when you stop at a traffic light, you can take a breath, exhale, and think "relax." Then you can do this every time you stop your car. You could also do this exercise every time you take a drink from a cup or every time you close a document on your computer. If you do this activity over and over, after a while, you will find that it occurs in a wide variety of situations, and it will be available to you to use on a moment's notice.

Homework

- Continue reading your MVA aloud on a daily basis, and record the number of times you read it each day. At this point, you may decrease the number of times you read the description to once per day.

- Continue your travel exposure exercises, remembering to user relaxation, corrective self-talk, and cognitive reappraisal.

- Use cue-controlled relaxation a minimum of 12 times per day, and rate your level of relaxation.

Chapter 11 *Sessions 7 Through 9*

This point often marks a shift in the focus of treatment. Now, your therapist is working with you to individualize your treatment. Perhaps you are feeling cut off from your feelings (what we term "psychic numbing") or you are experiencing a persistent fear of death. Maybe you feel estranged from others and socially isolated. You may even be experiencing difficulty controlling your anger.

In the next three sessions (sessions 7–9), you will work with your therapist to address any of these issues that may be troubling you.

Records Review

Review of your homework exercises is a part of every session. As you progress through the treatment, some tasks may not be as important to complete as they were earlier in the program (e.g., reading your MVA description, driving as part of your exposure exercises). Your therapist will provide guidance.

Depression, Social Isolation, and Psychic Numbing

Survivors of MVAs often begin to savor life in a different way. Even though lingering injuries may bother them, survivors are all too aware that they might not be alive if circumstances had been different. An MVA can greatly change one's life.

Responses to these changes can vary, influenced, in part, by individual differences between people. Friends, family, and personal beliefs shape us all. Many accident victims withdraw from their friends and family. They become more isolated. This isolation can contribute to a feeling of depression and a sense of hopelessness. It is often a part of their social isolation. As part of our recommendations, we have drawn on the work of early psychologists who studied depression. They found that social isolation and estrangement can be greatly helped by a direct approach, similar to exposure, and by increasing the number of positive events in an individual's life. This rather simplistic idea has turned out to be quite powerful. Friends, families, and pleasurable activities are important parts of life. However, much like avoidance of stressful situations, the need to deal with the complexities of relationships and a sense of not feeling up to being pleasant company can draw some people away from the very things that can be helpful.

As a way to counteract the estrangement and depression that can occur after an MVA, we have subsequently asked people to engage in activities on a regular basis that they used to find enjoyable or meaningful. Thus, while you may be doing a driving exercise to increase the number of hours and distance that you drive, it is certainly reasonable to end the activity with a pleasant lunch or another activity with a friend or family member. The pleasure that can come from these activities can help to minimize the distress and effort involved in the task and also can help you to address deeper concerns about who you are and why you are here on earth.

Often, people have explanations and excuses for avoiding friends and family, such as not feeling up to the task or waiting until they feel better. Although these excuses certainly can have some validity, they are often ways to cover up the avoidance that is part of the problem. At first, people may not feel the joy that they think should be part of the activities. Again, we encourage them to be patient and persistent. If they continue to do things that they used to enjoy, sooner or later, they will begin to enjoy them again. In essence, rather than waiting until you feel better before you try to do something that you used to enjoy, the answer is the reverse. Doing something that you used to enjoy (but have given up) will help you to feel better. Just as our thoughts direct our feelings, so do activities that we enjoy, particularly those that have particular importance and meaning. Do not underestimate the importance of the positive events that were part of your life in the past. Try to pursue them as best as circumstances allow.

The pleasant events list shown on page 90 is a brief compilation of activities that may or may not be enjoyable for you right now. It is provided to help stimulate your range of interests. Use this form to make a list of events that you once enjoyed or that you think you might enjoy now. Look at this list each day, and try to select at least one event that you can do that day. Try not to let a day go by without doing something that is potentially pleasant for you. It's often possible to combine two activities, such as driving (part of your hierarchy) and a purposeful, pleasant event (e.g., having lunch with a friend). Try to be creative, and make a real effort to see how this approach can work for you. The pleasant events practice sheet on page 91 can be used to keep track of your progress.

Pleasant Events List

Most people find that there are a number of events or activities that leave them feeling happier or more positive. The Pleasant Events list on page 90 shows a variety of activities that many people enjoy. There is space provided for you to add activities that you have enjoyed in the past or that you think might be enjoyable now. Try to identify one or more activities that you could begin to add to your day on a regular basis. Try to schedule at least one pleasant event each day. Good luck!

Pleasant Events Practice Sheet

The Pleasant Events Practice Sheet on page 91 is designed to help you incorporate enjoyable activities into your daily life. On the lines provided on the left, list 1 to 15 events or activities that you might find enjoyable or fun. Then, in the spaces on the right, record the date that you complete each event. Try to plan at least one pleasant event per day.

Fear of Death

One of the most dominant themes found among MVA survivors is the fear of death, accompanied by intrusive reminders of one's own mortality. Your accident may have changed your perspective on life. Life has become something not to be taken for granted. You may not want to fill your time with too many events during the day. You learned all too well that, in a moment, those things could change. The change can occur without any warning and without any responsibility or fault on your part. This change often causes people to question why these events occur and what they mean. In the last few sessions, it may be important to spend time soul-searching and thinking about these questions. Your accident can give you a chance to reorganize and refocus your life. You can examine your priorities and make important changes in your daily life.

Pleasant Events

1. Going to lunch with a friend
2. Speaking to a friend on the telephone
3. Going to a movie
4. Relaxing in a park or backyard
5. Reading a book for pleasure
6. Going for a walk with a friend or partner
7. Going out for ice cream on a warm evening
8. Attending a play or show
9. Playing a game with a child or friend
10. Having a special meal or treat
11.
12.
13.
14.
15.

Pleasant Events Practice Sheet

Event	Monday	Tuesday	Wednesday	Thursday	Friday	Saturday	Sunday
1.							
2.							
3.							
4.							
5.							
6.							
7.							
8.							
9.							
10.							
11.							
12.							
13.							
14.							
15.							

Once again, the act of taking charge of your life and reclaiming it, rather than being a victim, is important. As you came to understand how your thoughts and appraisals affect your actions, this same understanding can be applied to your philosophy and faith. Survivors have often found that their MVA, rather than being a detriment, has helped them to pursue the life that they desired. In many cases, MVAs have helped survivors to become better organized and to address the priorities and goals that they truly wish to meet with the time that they have in this life. MVAs have even helped people in their search for meaning in their existence.

Anger

Anger often occurs after an MVA. Patients do not feel as if they have done anything wrong and are uncertain at times whether to feel angry with the other driver, the weather, or even God.

It is important to understand that there certainly are events that can be anger-provoking. Some situations are so frustrating that indignation and anger will naturally occur. However, these cases are relatively rare, and you need to decide how you will choose to react to the many less serious situations that you will encounter. Exposure to anger-provoking situations and phrases can help you to develop mastery of your anger by applying other ways of thinking and reacting. To help you practice dealing with your anger using CBT, a worksheet has been provided for you on pages 93–94.

Homework *(may vary for sessions)*

- Continue to do the exposure exercises.
- Complete and utilize the pleasant events form.
- Complete any other assignment that you and your therapist have decided would be helpful (e.g., regarding mortality or anger).
- Complete the end-of-treatment assessment, and bring the results to your next session (session 10).
- Keep records of all of your homework assignments using the homework diary.

Anger Situations Worksheet

You can use the following situations to practice how you might deal with frustration and anger by changing either your initial reactions or your subsequent reactions.

Situation 1. While you are driving, another driver comes up behind you, tailgates for several minutes, pulls around you and angrily gives you the finger, and then pulls in front of you and slows down.

Describe your thoughts, possible ways to deal with the situation, and your ideas for how to prevent it from happening again.

_____
_____
_____
_____
_____

Situation 2. You are asked to undergo an independent medical examination. You just had a number of examinations by your own doctor, and you wonder why they just can't take your doctor's test results and opinions as they are intended. You don't want to have this examination, and you are afraid that it will mean cutting off your disability funds and a decision that will negatively affect your life.

Describe your reaction.

_____
_____
_____
_____
_____

How could you challenge your thoughts about this situation?

_____
_____
_____
_____
_____

Anger Situations Worksheet *continued*

Situation 3. You don't feel well. Your neck has been bothering you all day. Medication has not helped the pain, and you slept poorly the night before. Your child comes in from school very excitedly and jumps on your lap. This produces more pain. You have told your child many times to be careful around you because of your injuries, but he or she does not seem to listen.

What is your initial reaction?

What are your thoughts?

What are some possible alternative thoughts?

What are some possible alternative reactions?

Answers to Anger Situations Worksheet

Situation 1

Your immediate thought: "This jerk is dangerous. He has no business doing this: I need to take care of him before he hurts me. What an idiot!"

You can prevent these thoughts: "Okay, this guy is a bad driver, is it worth getting in a fight over it? Even if I stop him, there are more bad drivers out there."

Contol yourself and take a deep breath: "He'll be gone in a minute, and I can get back to my driving."

Situation 2

Your immediate reaction might be to feel anger, fear, and anxiety.

You can challenge your thoughts: "This is just an independent medical examination. I don't know how it's going to turn out. I have a lot of good doctors who are in my corner, trying to get me better. Whatever this person does, good or bad, I can deal with it. I don't have to catastrophize the outcome before anything really even happens."

Situation 3

Your initial reaction might be anger, and you might think, "I don't need this. This is too much. I can't take any more of this!"

Possible alternative thoughts and reactions could be one or both of the following:

"It's been a bad day. I've dealt with this before. The pain does change. Let's try to relax and use whatever I can to help me cope."

"Kids don't always listen That's why they're kids. It would have been better if he hadn't jumped on me and hurt me, but I'm glad he loves me. Maybe I need to figure out another way to get him to listen more often. We've got time. It hurt, but I'll survive."

Chapter 12 *End-of-Treatment Reassessment*

End-of-Treatment Reassessment

It's now time to see how well you're doing. The assessment instruments that you completed at the start and in the middle of treatment will be used again. This chapter provides another blank copy of the questionnaires that you completed at those times. After you complete them once more, please go back and compare your answers with the questionnaires that you answered at the beginning and at the middle of your treatment. Take this new set of questionnaires to session 10 to review with your therapist.

Posttraumatic Stress Disorder

First, let's check the symptoms of PTSD. The PCL is provided again for that purpose (see page 98).

To complete the PCL, just answer the questions in terms of how you've been feeling over the past week. Total your answers, and compare them with your earlier tests.

Depression

Once again, we've provided you with a copy of the CES-D (page 99). Take the questionnaire, completing the items in terms of how you've felt over the past week. Then look back on your earlier questionnaire and see how you did. Take the completed questionnaire to session 10.

Travel Anxiety

The last area to look at is your fear and anxiety about travel. Again, unlike the other questionnaires, this questionnaire doesn't have a set of numbers for easy comparison, but you can certainly look back at how you answered the questions on the TAQ before (page 100).

Current Posttraumatic Stress Disorder Checklist (PCL)

Name: _____ Date: _____

Instructions: Following is a list of problems and complaints that people sometimes have in response to stressful life experiences (i.e., your most distressing MVA). Please read each one carefully, and then circle one of the numbers to the right to indicate how much you have been bothered by that problem and by your most distressful MVA in the **past week**.

	Not at All	A Little Bit	Moderately	Quite a Bit	Extremely
1. Repeated, disturbing memories, thoughts, or images of the stressful experience?	1	2	3	4	5
2. Repeated, disturbing dreams of the stressful experience?	1	2	3	4	5
3. Suddenly acting or feeling as if the stressful experience were happening again (as if you were reliving it)?	1	2	3	4	5
4. Feeling very upset when something reminded you of the stressful experience?	1	2	3	4	5
5. Having a physical reaction (e.g., heart pounding, trouble breathing, sweating) when something reminded you of the stressful experience?	1	2	3	4	5
6. Avoiding thinking about or talking about your stressful experience or avoiding having feelings related to it?	1	2	3	4	5
7. Avoiding activities or situations because they reminded you of your stressful experience?	1	2	3	4	5
8. Trouble remembering important parts of the stressful experience?	1	2	3	4	5
9. Loss of interest in activities that you used to enjoy?	1	2	3	4	5
10. Feeling distant or cut off from others?	1	2	3	4	5
11. Feeling emotionally numb or being unable to have loving feelings for those close to you?	1	2	3	4	5
12. Feeling as if your future somehow will be cut short?	1	2	3	4	5
13. Trouble falling or staying asleep?	1	2	3	4	5
14. Feeling irritable or having angry outbursts?	1	2	3	4	5
15. Having difficulty concentrating?	1	2	3	4	5
16. Being "super-alert," watchful, or on guard?	1	2	3	4	5
17. Feeling jumpy or easily startled?	1	2	3	4	5
Total					

Current Center for Epidemiologic Studies–Depression (CES-D)

Name: _____   Date: _____

For each statement, please circle the number that best describes how often you have felt or behaved this way during the **past week**.

	Rarely or None of the Time	Some or a Little of the Time	Occasionally or a Moderate Amount of the Time	Most or All of the Time
I was bothered by things that usually don't bother me	0	1	2	3
I did not feel like eating; my appetite was poor	0	1	2	3
I felt like I could not shake off the blues, even with help from my family or friends	0	1	2	3
I felt like I was just as good as other people	0	1	2	3
I had trouble keeping my mind on what I was doing	0	1	2	3
I felt depressed	0	1	2	3
I felt that everything I did was an effort	0	1	2	3
I felt hopeful about the future	0	1	2	3
I thought my life had been a failure	0	1	2	3
I felt fearful	0	1	2	3
My sleep was restless	0	1	2	3
I was happy	0	1	2	3
I talked less than usual	0	1	2	3
I felt lonely	0	1	2	3
People were unfriendly	0	1	2	3
I enjoyed life	0	1	2	3
I had crying spells	0	1	2	3
I felt sad	0	1	2	3
I felt like people disliked me	0	1	2	3
I could not get "going"*	0	1	2	3
I had thoughts about my death	0	1	2	3
I thought about harming myself	0	1	2	3
Sum of scores				
Total score =				

*Stop scoring after this item.

Travel Anxiety Questionnaire (TAQ)

Name: _____ Date: _____

1. Are you driving at the **present** time? (Circle one)
   1. Yes Go to question 3
   2. No   Continue to question 2

2. If you are *not* driving presently, why not? (Check *all* that apply)
   - ☐ Driving makes me anxious
   - ☐ Physically unable
   - ☐ No car
   - ☐ No license
   - ☐ None of the above

3. Following are eight driving situations. Use the two scales below to **rate how anxious** you are about each situation currently, as well as **how much you avoid** each of these situations **currently**. If the situation does not apply to you, please circle "NA" next to the situation.

   Anxiety rating scale

   0 ——————— 1 ——————— 2 ——————— 3 ——————— 4

   No anxiety / Very little anxiety / Some anxiety / Moderate anxiety / Severe anxiety

   Avoidance rating acale

   0 ——————— 1 ——————— 2 ——————— 3 ——————— 4

   None of the time / Less than half of the time / About half of the time / More than half of the time / All of the time

	Anxiety rating	Avoidance rating	
Driving at night	_____	_____	NA
Driving in snow	_____	_____	NA
Driving in rain	_____	_____	NA
Highway driving	_____	_____	NA
Driving in heavy traffic	_____	_____	NA
Driving in the location of the MVA	_____	_____	NA
Driving on pleasure trips	_____	_____	NA
Being the passenger	_____	_____	NA

Please circle either yes or no:

4. **Currently,** do you restrict your driving speed?   Yes   No

5. **Currently,** do you drive only to work?   Yes   No

Summary

We hope that this reassessment will help you to see the progress you're making and realize how far you've come. The questionnaires allow you to measure changes in anxiety (PTSD), mood (depression), and fear and anxiety about driving (travel anxiety). The goal is to get better. This information can help you to target any remaining difficulties and help you to decide what you need to do to overcome them.

Chapter 13

Session 10
Termination Session

Overview

By this point, you've done a lot of work, and we hope that you're feeling better.

To see how you're doing, your therapist will be reviewing your particular areas of focus over the past few weeks, which may include the following:

- Numbing and estrangement
- Anger
- Mortality
- Ongoing medical injury
- Depression
- Symptoms of trauma and anxiety

Records Review

Once again, you and your therapist will review your homework assignments.

Review of the End-of-Treatment Assessment (PCL, CES-D, and TAQ)

At this point, you and your therapist will discuss the need for additional treatment. If further treatment is needed, you will set goals for the additional sessions. If further treatment is not needed, you and your therapist will schedule a 1-month follow-up appointment, telephone follow-up, or both, to keep track of your progress.

You've gone through a lot, and you've done a lot of hard work. You've learned to use a number of new tools that you can apply to your reactions to your accident, as well as to other areas of your life. You've learned to use relaxation techniques that can help you in a variety of situations, such as when you're feeling anxious, when you have trouble sleeping, when you're stuck in traffic, and when you feel overwhelmed. You've learned how to use a number of cognitive tools, including coping self-statements and cognitive reappraisal. You have also learned how your thoughts affect how you feel and what you do, and you've practiced methods for changing automatic, irrational thoughts. You've also addressed areas that you've been avoiding as a way to help deal with your anxiety and fears. You've learned how powerful avoidance was, as well as how powerful you can be, as you deal with your fears more directly, either in real life, as with your travel anxiety hierarchy, or with imaginal exposure, as you addressed the thoughts and images in your head. Congratulations! That's hard to do, and you've done a lot to get this far.

You've probably also had to deal with other psychological aftermath of your accident, including anger, feeling changed and different, and having to rejoin the world, even after it was changed by the trauma of your crash. It's been hard work, but you should feel stronger as a result of doing the work, and you should be able to recognize the courage that it takes to succeed.

You and your therapist will review your progress. If it's time to stop treatment, that's great! If there's more work to do, that's okay. You will be able to see it for what it is and establish a plan for how to accomplish all of your goals.

This book has outlined a 10-session treatment for psychological difficulties resulting from a MVA. Not everyone finishes his or her treatment in 10 sessions. In our studies, the range of sessions needed was between 7 and 12. We have found that the tenth session is often a good place to reassess what symptoms or problems continue and to agree to a therapeutic plan for addressing these concerns.

The number of treatment sessions is perhaps less important than teaching you the skills to deal with the problems in a way that can give you a good chance of succeeding. A good working relationship between you and your therapist is an important part of this process. And for those clients interested in further reading on this topic, we direct you to the references section at the back of this workbook, where you will find a representative sampling of related professional articles and books.

Good Luck!

References and Suggestions for Further Reading

Alexander, D. (1999). The presentation of adult symptoms. In E. J. Hickling & E. B. Blanchard (Eds.), *International handbook of road traffic accidents & psychological trauma: Current understanding, treatment & law* (pp. 1–14). Amsterdam: Elsevier.

American Psychiatric Association. (1994). *Diagnostic and statistical manual of mental disorders* (4th ed.). Washington, DC: Author.

Blanchard, E. B., & Hickling, E. J. (2004). *After the crash: Assessment and treatment of motor vehicle accident survivors* (2nd ed.). Washington, DC: American Psychological Association.

Blanchard, E. B., Hickling, E. B., Barton, K. A., Taylor, A. E., Loos, W. R., & Jones-Alexander, J. (1996). One-year prospective follow-up of motor vehicle accident victims. *Behaviour Research and Therapy, 34,* 775–786.

Blanchard, E. B., Hickling, E. J., Devineni, T., Veazey, C. H., Galovski, T. E., Mundy, E., et al. (2003). A controlled evaluation of cognitive-behavioral therapy for posttraumatic stress in motor vehicle accident survivors. *Behaviour Research and Therapy, 41,* 79–96.

Blanchard, E. B., Hickling, E. J., Mitnick, N., Taylor, A. E., Loos, W. R., & Buckley, T. C. (1995). The impact of severity of physical injury and perception of life threat in the development of post-traumatic stress disorder in motor vehicle accident victims. *Journal of Traumatic Stress, 11,* 337–354.

Blanchard, E. B., Hickling, E. J., Taylor, A. E., Loos, W. R., & Forneris, C. A. (1996). Who develops PTSD from motor vehicle accidents? *Behaviour Research and Therapy, 34,* 1–10.

Breslau, N., Davis, G. C., Andreski, P., & Peterson, E. (1991). Traumatic events and post-traumatic stress disorder in an urban population of young adults. *Archives of General Psychiatry, 48,* 216–222.

Bryant, R. A., & Harvey, A. G. (2000). *Acute stress disorder: A handbook of theory, assessment and treatment.* Washington, DC: American Psychological Association Books.

Bryant, R. A., Harvey, A. G., Dang, S. T., Sackville, T., & Basten, C. (1998). Treatment of acute stress disorder: A comparison of cognitive-behavioral therapy and supportive counseling. *Journal of Consulting and Clinical Psychology, 66,* 862–866.

Bryant, R. A., Moulds, M. L., & Gutherie, R. M. (2000). Acute stress disorder scale: A self-report measure of acute stress disorder. *Psychological Assessment, 12,* 61–68.

Bryant, R. A., Sackville, T., Dang, S. T., Moulds, M., & Guthrie, R. (1999). Treating acute stress disorder: An evaluation of cognitive behavior therapy and supportive counseling techniques. *American Journal of Psychiatry, 156,* 1780–1786.

Buckley, T. C., Blanchard, E. B., & Hickling, E. J. (1996). A prospective examination of delayed onset PTSD secondary to motor vehicle accidents. *Journal of Abnormal Psychology, 105,* 617–625.

Ehlers, A., Mayou, R. A., & Bryant, B. (1998). Psychological predictors of chronic posttraumatic stress disorder after motor vehicle accidents. *Journal of Abnormal Psychology, 107,* 508–519.

Fein, M. L. (1993). *I. A. M. (Integrated anger management): A common sense guide to coping with anger.* Westport, CT: Praeger.

Harvey, A. G., & Bryant, A. G. (1998). The relationship between acute stress disorder and posttraumatic stress disorder: A prospective evaluation of motor vehicle accident survivors. *Journal of Consulting and Clinical Psychology, 66,* 507–512.

Hickling, E. J., & Blanchard, E. B. (1992). Post-traumatic stress disorder and motor vehicle accidents. *Journal of Anxiety Disorders, 6,* 283–304.

Hickling, E. J., & Blanchard, E. B. (1997). The private practice psychologist and manual-based treatment: A case study in the treatment of post-traumatic stress disorder secondary to motor vehicle accidents. *Behaviour Research and Therapy, 35,* 191–203.

Hickling, E. J., & Blanchard, E. B. (Eds.). (1999). *International handbook of road traffic accidents and psychological trauma: Current understanding, treatment, and law.* New York: Elsevier.

Hickling, E. J., Blanchard, E. B., Buckley, T. C., & Taylor, A. E. (1999). Effects of attribution of responsibility for motor vehicle accidents on severity of PTSD symptoms. *Journal of Traumatic Stress, 12*(2), 345–353.

Hickling, E. J., Sison, G. F. P., & Vanderploeg, K. D. (1986). The treatment of posttraumatic stress disorder with biofeedback and relaxation training. *Biofeedback and Self-Regulation, 11,* 125–134.

Mayou, R., Ehlers, A., & Bryant, R. (2002). Posttraumatic stress disorder after motor vehicle accidents: 3 year follow-up of a prospective longitudinal study. *Behaviour Research and Therapy, 40,* 665–675.

McKay, M., Rogers, P. D., & McKay, J. (1989). *When anger hurts: Quieting the storm within.* Oakland, CA: New Harbinger.

Novaco, R. W. (1975). *Anger control: The development and evaluation of an experimental treatment.* Lexington, MA: Lexington Books.

Radloff, L. S. (1977). The CES-D scale: A self-report depression scale for research in the general population. *Applied Psychological Measurement, 1,* 385–401.

U.S. National Highway Traffic Safety Administration. (2002, December). *Traffic safety facts 2000: A compilation of motor vehicle crash data from the fatal accident reporting system and general estimates system* (DOT HS 809 337). Washington, DC: U.S. Department of Transportation.

U.S. National Highway Traffic Safety Administration. *2004 annual assessment: Crash fatality counts and injury estimates* [Data file]. Available from National Highway Traffic Safety Administration Web site, www.transportation.gov

Weathers, F., Litz, B. T., Herman, D. S., Huska, J. A., & Keane, T. M. (1993). *The PTSD checklist: Reliability, validity & diagnostic utility.* Paper presented at the annual meeting of the International Society for Traumatic Stress Studies, San Antonio, TX.

Wolpe, J. (1962). Isolation of a conditioning procedure as the crucial psychotherapeutic factor: A case study. *Journal of Nervous and Mental Disease, 134,* 316–329.

About the Authors

Edward J. Hickling, PsyD, received his doctorate in clinical psychology from the University of Denver, School of Professional Psychology, in 1982. He worked as the Director of Training and as a consultation liaison psychologist at the Veteran's Administration Medical Center in Albany, New York, until 1987, when he left to enter full-time private practice. In addition to his practice in clinical psychology, he holds positions as an adjunct professor at the State University of New York, Albany, in the Psychology Department, and is on the clinical faculty at the Albany Medical College, Department of Psychiatry. He has collaborated with Edward Blanchard and has held the position of Senior Research Scientist at the Center for Stress and Anxiety Disorders since 1990, when he became the Co-Principal Investigator on several National Institute of Mental Health–funded grants investigating the psychological impact of motor vehicle accidents. Hickling has published more than 70 papers and several books, including two co-authored with Edward Blanchard on their work with motor vehicle accident survivors, *After the Crash: Assessment and Treatment of Motor Vehicle Accident Survivors,* and the edited volume, *International Handbook of Road Traffic Accidents and Psychological Trauma: Current Understanding, Treatment, and Law.* Current interests include innovative treatments (very brief therapy and online applications) for posttraumatic stress disorder, behavioral medicine, and psychological interventions in integrative and complementary medicine.

Edward B. Blanchard, PhD, ABPP, received his doctoral degree in clinical psychology from Stanford University in 1969. After brief stints at the University of Georgia (1969–1971), the University of Mississippi Medical Center (1971–1975), and the University of Tennessee Center for the Health Sciences in Memphis (1975–1977), he came to the University of Albany in 1977 as Professor and Director of Clinical Training. He was named Distinguished Professor of Psychology in 1989. In 2004, he retired and became Distinguished Professor Emeritus of Psychology. He has held National Institutes of Health grants in assessment and cognitive-behavioral treatments for headache, hypertension, and irritable bowel syndrome. His work on posttraumatic stress disorder began in the early 1980s, with an initial focus on Vietnam War veterans. Since 1989, he has collaborated with Edward Hickling on research on survivors of serious motor vehicle accidents. His work on this topic was supported by grants from the National Institute of Mental Health and forms the background for this book.

CPSIA information can be obtained at www.ICGtesting.com
Printed in the USA
BVOW05s1355131113

336204BV00001B/17/P